HOUSE & GARDEN'S
BEST IN DECORATION

HOUSE & GARDEN'S
BEST IN
DECORATION

By the Editors of House & Garden

Condé Nast Books
Random House
New York

All rights reserved under International
and Pan-American Copyright Conventions.
Published in the United States
by Random House, Inc., New York,
and simultaneously in Canada
by Random House of Canada, Limited, Toronto.

Library of Congress
Cataloging-in-Publication Data

House & Garden's Best In Decoration
    1. Interior decoration—History—20th century.
I. House & Garden. II. House and Garden's Best In Decoration.
NK1980.H63   1987   747.2'049   87-42643
ISBN 0-394-56426-X

Frontispiece: John Saladino's New York apartment.
Opposite: Detail of Carolyn Farb's house in Houston,
decorated by McMillen.

PROJECT STAFF

For Condé Nast Books
Jill Cohen, *Director*
Jonathan E. Newhouse, *Special Consultant*
Ellen Maria Bruzelius, *Project Manager*
Kristine Smith, *Project Assistant*
Diane Pesce, *Composition Manager*
Peter Bakker, *Color Control and Print Production*

For House & Garden Magazine
Louis O. Gropp, *Editor-in-Chief*
Alice Gordon, *Project Editor*

*Produced in association
with Media Projects Incorporated*
Carter Smith, *Executive Editor*
Judy Knipe, *Project Manager*
Charlotte McGuinn Freeman, *Permissions Editor*
Ann Harakawa, *Designer*

Special thanks is made
to the following individuals at *House & Garden* Magazine:
Senior Editors, Elaine Greene, Babs Simpson
Decorating Editors, Jacqueline Gonnet,
Karen Parker Gray, and Carolyn Sollis
Contributing Editor, Dorothea Walker
Picture Editor, Thomas H. McWilliam Jr.
Assistant to the Editor-in-Chief, Jill Citron

Contents

Introduction

*A*t *House & Garden* we take decoration very seriously. So seriously, in fact, that in the early 1980s we literally recreated the magazine, then over eighty years old, to better tell decoration's story. Observing important developments in our society—more equality between the sexes, more specialized education and technology, more affluence, and more pluralism—we came to the conclusion that our own special audience was ready for a magazine of new depth and intelligence, daring and creativity, a journal to promote an even fuller understanding of decoration and design, art and architecture, and how they pertain to our rapidly changing lives.

We decided to take on this assignment with a single-minded emphasis on quality: materially, through the paper and ink we used: editorially, through our subject matter and its presentation; intellectually, through new approaches to photography, a commitment to literary content, and a closer study of our culture. To live a life of quality today is not easy, if it ever was; good and bad live in close proximity, colliding in the sometimes ambivalent lives of each of us. To empower our audience for creative living in all its many aspects became the magazine's larger goal. In moving toward that objective we have criticized false comfort, but more often we find ourselves celebrating the things that bring us closer to the good life we all want to live. *House & Garden's Best in Decoration* is about our celebrations.

This selection of interiors deals with the signs and symbols of movement toward the good life as they are reflected in the highly creative world of decoration. Always about things, decoration is now more than ever about people too—both the people who create rooms and the people who live in them. Many of the decorators and clients in this book live life on the fast track, creating and absorbing overnight the kind of influences that used to be years in the forming. They send us the "high style" of European capitals and usher in a new American appreciation for richness of color, pattern, and texture; at the same time, they look to areas, like Japan, that for too long have been ignored by the West and they find entirely new connotations of serenity and elegance in the play of white on white. By embracing such opposites, professionals and patrons suggest the largest possible range of decorating for everyone.

      With so much variety in the world of decoration, there cannot be a *House & Garden* "look" for people to copy. The last thing we want to offer you is a formula for successful decorating. Instead, we want to open up possibilities, create options, trigger ideas, and inspire individual choice—including the choice of looking at these pages not with intentions of emulation or ownership but with simple pleasure at their beauty and information.

      House & Garden's Best in Decoration is not only about what decoration has to say about life today but about the life that can be found in today's decoration. We think it bears witness most powerfully to the fact that taste and style are certainly not static, and that the enormous energy and insight available to us makes room for every kind of expression. This book was created with the conviction that its readers are like its creators: curious, passionately interested in the arts, concerned about the quality of life, desirous of living with beauty, appreciative of the best the world has to offer, and always ready to enhance a special world of their own.

Louis Oliver Gropp
Editor-in-Chief, House & Garden

Part I
Designers and Clients

What is it exactly that gives interior decorators the ability to show other people how to live? There is the elusive "taste," of course, and, in different measure, a love of rooms and how they function; a fascination with objects and why people have them; an appreciation of composition, color, shape, line, texture, proportion, pattern, light, shadow, and how they can effect a mood or attitude; a sense of history and an idea of the future. This first part of *House & Garden's Best in Decoration* celebrates the designer's spirit of investigation, that which finds a way to turn intangible "home" into reality within four walls.

Exploring the work of top international designers helps reveal how a client's varying needs and desires generate a decorator's creativity. The simple preferences in color and materials that the jewelry designer Elsa Peretti gave to Renzo Mongiardino—"master of ambience"—signified to him a "patchwork of antiquity" that would reflect her native city of Rome. The publishing executive Christopher Whittle's decision to move from a two-room log cabin in Tennessee to a historic apartment building "representing everything Manhattan had to offer" inspired Peter Marino to recast Whittle's rooms in the Dakota with their original, staggering turn-of-the-century opulence. Former Ambassador Anne Cox Chambers's utter trust and admiration of the easy way her scholarly friend Roderick Cameron "conjugated knowledge with the business of living" led her to ask him for the kind of remarkable rooms he would have made for himself.

Remarkable decorators know how to follow the lead of remarkable architecture. Under the supervision of Piero Pinto, the fifteenth-century castle that the fashion designer Laura Biagiotti fell in love with became "a tangible testimony to art and history." San Franciscan Harry Hunt's lucky purchase of one of the city's important modern buildings meant that the French designer Andrée Putman could in her clean-lined decoration pay tribute to the very reasons modernism came about. On the other hand, because the architecture in Bill Blass's apartment was *not* remarkable, Mac II gave the rooms "good bones" before dressing them in the crisp aesthetic that defines the designer's classic clothes.

Career or calling will often figure in the way a designer approaches decorating for a particular client. Oscar de la Renta, whose romantic dresses are designed for the kind of parties he hosts himself, was given by Denning & Fourcade romantic rooms where "lights form mysterious constellations" and walls offset "jeweled women in jewel-colored dresses." Mario Buatta's "English-casual-relaxed" environment for Taki Theodoracopulos's American brownstone provided all the coziness and peacefulness the writer required. Ashton Hawkins, the general counsel to The Metropolitan Museum of Art, wanted to be able to leave his work at "the office" but still enjoy a personal art collection at home. Mark Hampton's subtle backdrop allowed Hawkins's art to be "the real furnishings of the apartment," thus creating an intimate gallery for living.

Art was also behind Geoffrey Bennison's splendid sets for the theatrical elements of *le style Rothschild,* Antony Childs's graceful melding of residence and baroque-art gallery for the dealer Ramon Osuna in Washington, and Bruce Gregga's boldly colored scheme for Betsy and Andrew Rosenfield, collectors of contemporary painting and sculpture and early-modern furniture. But it was actually the deaccessioning of an important art collection that made Enid Annenberg Haupt, a veteran tastemaker, hire a decorator for the very first time. When Mrs. Haupt brought in the incomparable Sister Parish to reappoint her New York penthouse apartment, she discovered what we hope the following pages will reaffirm for you: that decoration is an art one can live with very well.

Geoffrey Bennison for the Baron and Baroness Guy de Rothschild

*A*s patrons of the decorative arts, the Rothschilds took over where royalty left off. For over a century their town houses, châteaux, hunting lodges, stud farms, and villas were the envy of western Europe; and to this day, *le style Rothschild* signifies everything that is most precious and fastidious in art and decoration, largely thanks to Marie-Hélène de Rothschild, the charismatic and infinitely discriminating wife of the Baron Guy.

Marie-Hélène has presided over the beautification of one great house after another, from a sixteenth-century *manoir* outside Deauville to her husband's ancestral château, Ferrières, to what is probably the finest seventeenth-century house in Paris—Le Vau's Hôtel Lambert, the pride and, thanks to its situation, the prow of the Île Saint-Louis. On the score of sheer sumptuousness the Hôtel Lambert would appear to be an impossible act to follow, let alone equal. But trust Marie-Hélène to bring off the impossible. She conjured up a Xanadu—an Orientalist folly of incomparable magic—in an oasis outside Marrakesh. And the project you see here—the decoration with Geoffrey Bennison of an off-beat apartment on New York's Upper East Side—is also a triumph, albeit of a very different order: Marie-Hélène has succeeded against all the odds in trans-

planting her own inimitable Parisian style and atmosphere to Manhattan.

When the Rothschilds set about house-hunting in New York, friends automatically assumed that Marie-Hélène would settle in a conventional Park Avenue or Fifth Avenue apartment. Not on your life. Everything she was shown she found "banal, characterless, or low-ceilinged." Finally she was offered an unconventional duplex in an unconventional landmark building (architect: Charles Adams Platt). "A modest front door opening off a modest hallway hardly prepared me for the great space within," she says. "The living room had a twenty-foot ceiling and as much light as an artist's studio. *C'était le coup de foudre.* What a relief to find something with character and scale. At last I had the feeling of being in a house instead of an apartment. My New York friends said I was crazy to buy it."

The friends have had to eat their words. For Marie-Hélène and Geoffrey Bennison—canniest of decorators when it comes to reading a client's mind—have succeeded in creating what, those who have seen it feel, is the most spectacular apartment of its kind in New York, a landmark in modern decorating to the extent that it is the quintessence of "high style." Intentionally or not, they make us forget that we are in the United States and transport us in imagination to a comfortable château somewhere in the Île de France, one that has remained unchanged since the turn of the century.

Above: *In the salon, busts of Roman emperors on their original ebony stands, from the Great Hall at Ferrières. Between them, a 17th-century Italian cabinet of ebony and pietra dura.* Opposite: *A Boulle clock from Ferrières flanked by two 17th-century silver gilt goblets made in Augsburg.*

Marie-Hélène knows just how to set the stage for herself. Her subtle sense of drama is exemplified by the way she has played down the entrance hall (intricate arrangements of eighteenth-century engravings are the only concession to decoration), the better to stun you with your first glimpse of the spectacular salon that opens off it. Despite its vast height and grandiose contents (not least the palatial busts from Ferrières), despite the flamboyant "paneling" that Bennison has painted in imitation of the marquetry room at Hever Castle, the salon turns out to be warm and wonderfully welcoming.

The same is true of the library, into which one is lured by a glow of light emanating from behind heavy portières in the salon. This is a room that lives up to its name: burnished rows of calf-bound books and a desk complete with inkstand, pens and nibs, and sealing wax. The walls are painted a wonderful reddish color—which Bennison describes as "sanguine crayon"—and are covered with drawings, among them a family portrait by Ingres.

Off the library opens a dining room lined with antique panels of Indian crewelwork hung like wallpaper and held in place by a wide *galon* studded with lozenges of bronze. So eye-catching is the effect that one almost overlooks the marvelous pair of unsigned Louis XV consoles.

Elsewhere on the ground floor is a separate guest suite: a smallish bedroom and an enchanting sitting room whose walls Bennison has covered in sepia striped velvet, "*gauffré* on linen, not silk," he says, "so as to look matte and unnew." The furniture is upholstered in Turkey carpet and string-colored fringe, and opposite the window hangs a group of fanciful watercolors by that rarest of naturalists, Aloys Zotl. These *recherché* works are a source of special pride to Marie-Hélène because they are not Rothschild heirlooms. The discovery, in her early twenties, of this cache is a measure of Marie-Hélène's connoisseurship.

Upstairs in the Baroness's characteristically *cossu* bedroom, one of Bennison's floral linens covers every surface except the floor, not least her extravagant Second Empire bed, which looks like a Rothschild heirloom but turns out to have an American provenance. Thanks to mahoganized paneling cluttered with memorabilia, the Baron's room is as masculine as his wife's is feminine, but both rooms look as if they had been brought over lock, stock, and barrel from one of the family's French houses. Between them, Marie-Hélène and Bennison are past masters at endowing a room with instant patina, instant nostalgia.

Easy enough, you might say, for a Rothschild to come up with a magnificent apartment. Has not Marie-

In the dining room, Victorian button leather chairs flank one of two unsigned Louis XV console tables. The metal horse under the 19th-century English needlework picture of a tiger, though it looks Renaissance, was probably a trade sign used by a blacksmith. The tablecloth and wall hangings are early-19th-century Indian crewelwork.

Hélène the advantage of an ancestral *garde meuble* whose contents are on par with the Musée des Arts Décoratifs? Can she not take her pick of signed commodes, Renaissance bronzes, some of the finest lace in private hands, and much more besides? True, most of the *objets de vertu* have the rarity and richness we expect from the Rothschilds. But anyone who studies the contents of this apartment will find that family treasures are the exception rather than the rule. Marie-Hélène has a prodigiously sharp and acquisitive eye, and many of the things that look like heirlooms—for instance, the beautiful Flemish chest ornamented with jewel-colored flowers—turn out to have been acquired specifically for the apartment. The same goes for most of the carpets.

And then take the voluptuously upholstered furniture—half the battle when it comes to evoking the atmosphere of the Second Empire. Some of the pieces, it is true, were made for Ferrières in the nineteenth century, but a lot has been executed to Marie-Hélène's or Bennison's specifications by Hervé de Larue, the *tapissier* she brought over from Paris. Likewise most of the antique textiles and the ubiquitous Victorian needlework actually comes from Bennison's unique stock. In the absence of anything suitable in his London emporium, the decorator adapted stuffs from old documents: for example, the faded-looking floral linen in the bedroom, which looks as if it had been there forever, was inspired by a fragment discovered in a noble nursery.

Bennison and the Baroness are at pains to give one another credit for the beauty of this apartment. Rightly so. Theirs is an expectionally close and creative collaboration, based as it is on mutual understanding and affection. "Marie-Hélène has more panache than anyone I know," says Bennison, "and her surroundings always reflect this. I wanted the apartment to capture this panache, also

her romanticism, her drama, her style. I envisaged the big room as a setting for a Balzac heroine, a grande dame who is a star but a *jeune fille* at heart. Marie-Hélène is a joy to work for because she knows exactly how to achieve it." As for Marie-Hélène, she allows that she derives the greatest satisfaction from working with Bennison: "Sometimes we fight like cat and dog, but we always end up seeing eye to eye—the best of friends." And unwittingly she echoes Bennison: "You see, he knows exactly what I want...."

It is no coincidence that Marie-Hélène has a preference for decorators who have trained as stage designers. Thanks to studying under Vladimir Polunin (one of Diaghilev's scene painters), Bennison knows how to evoke atmosphere, how to juggle with scale, and how to take advantage of the way certain colors and textures register at a distance—all-important when vast spaces are at stake. Look, for instance, how cleverly he has played up the height of the living room by hanging a seventeenth-century ebony mirror of gargantuan proportions way above the fireplace.

Bennison's eye for light and color and tone matches his feeling for scale. Particularly effective is the way he has dealt with the big north window: using acres of superb lace framed by gigantic William Morris curtains to

soften and contain the harsh light that streams through it; and the way he has used colors that are rich, warm, and resonant to take the chill off things. To the same ends considerable ingenuity has gone into the lighting: the library's golden gleam comes from minute bulbs concealed in the thickness of the bookshelves, and strategically adjusted lamps make for incandescence that recalls Georges de la Tour. That is why this apartment, for all its grandeur, is so *intime*, so flattering to the occupants. "Marie-Hélène and I like rooms that look welcoming and lived-in," says Bennison, "never intimidating, showy, or cold. You can be as grand as you like provided you know when to play things down."

The only problem, according to an American admirer of the apartment, is that you need a lot of style to live up to these rooms. There is some truth to this observation, and it explains why the Rothschild apartment is such a tempting and extremely difficult model to follow. Tempting, because it represents the quintessence of "high style"; difficult because it sets standards of quality and craftsmanship that in this day and age and in this country are virtually unattainable, and because the relationship between this charismatic patron and charismatic designer is too intuitive to duplicate.

In the Baroness's bedroom, walls and curtains are of a floral linen Bennison copied from a 19th-century document. Floral needlework panels cover the sofa. The gilt bed is Second Empire in the Rococo style.

Robert Bray and Michael Schaible for Arllyn and Alan L. Freeman

*T*he three best skyscraper apartment views in the United States are the Golden Gate Bridge on the West Coast, Central Park on the East Coast, and Chicago's lakeshore in between. These are views that make things happen. For example, when Arllyn and Alan L. Freeman's children were growing up and the couple felt it was time to look for a family weekend place that was totally urban, totally different from their suburban life of chintz and wallpaper and clutter and gardening, the prime requirement was that it center on the wondrous lakeshore view of Chicago's Gold Coast.

Their condominium was a hole in the ground when they bought a duplex above the fiftieth floor and began to look for an interior designer. Alan Freeman, commodities broker, yachtsman, and connoisseur of mechanical details, gladly took on the role of chief client which his wife equally gladly handed him; while the design process fascinates him, it bores her. (Results are something else: she loves what he has achieved.)

Alan Freeman likes to show interested visitors the model apartments still in place in his building because they demonstrate what he was trying to avoid: "little rooms leading into other little rooms. When you come in the

front door, you can't see the lake unless you look down a narrow hall and through a lot of furniture. You might as well be in Highland Park." The Freemans had to interview several interior designers in several cities who could only come up with "just another apartment" before they commissioned the New York team of Robert Bray and Michael Schaible.

Bray and Schaible perceived the location and the raw space the way Alan Freeman did, and there was not much more than that perception in the clients' program— except four bedrooms, places for two generations to entertain, easy maintenance, "and glamour." The architecture of the building did not interfere greatly with the interior designers, either. They were bound only by fixed plumbing stacks and some structural piers. No partitions were erected until they drew the plans, and the stairs were also placed by Bray-Schaible.

The apartment has a five-sided plan that might be viewed as a prow-ended figure pointing straight at Lake Michigan. Three of the five sides have windows, but the entry is deep in the core of the building and Bray-Schaible's handling of it instantly demonstrates their sympathy with the apartment's reason for being. Bob Bray says, "When you take a long ride in the elevator of a building in such a location you want to get to a window and look out as soon as you're in the door." Accordingly a path was paved from the foyer to the nearest lakeside window, and it passes between two enormous columns that look evocatively like a ship's smokestacks. One column holds a weight-bearing pier, the other carries plumbing pipes. In the building's more conventional apartments these elements were concealed in walls; here the vertical intrusions became a pair of forms that act like portals and contribute to a feeling of *being someplace,* not a given in this kind of slick tower.

Bray and Schaible used a few materials in huge amounts to create the strength and beauty of the interiors. Pinkish granite, twenty-eight tons of it, covers floors, makes tables, stairs, counters, low space dividers, column footings. A truckload of glass block went into numerous walls that admit light and bring a clear rough-smooth look, as much admired today as it was in the thirties. Most of the soft furnishings are gunmetal gray; most of the wall paint is creamy white. All of the detailing is meticulous.

Alan Freeman, connoisseur of mechanical matters, continues to admire the fixtures and the hardware, the way walls and ceilings are engineered so they will not crack when the building sways, the way he is protected against building noises. Arllyn Freeman says, "In winter we may look down at chunks of ice in the lake and stay indoors together; in summer there might be crowds of people in bright bathing suits on the beach and we'll run down and join them. We all feel like we have a wonderful hotel to come to every weekend."

The foyer, on the far side of the twin columns at left, is two shallow steps below the main-floor level and has a one-story ceiling, which helps build the drama of passing into the two-story part of the living room. Furniture by Bray-Schaible. Slipcovers are moiré from Manuel Canovas.

*Tucked into the center of
the lower floor is a
much-used video room
furnished with six
Corbusier chaises from ai;
I-beam tables by Ward
Bennett. Rounded wall of
glass block brings
daylight into the guest
powder room.*

Mario Buatta for Taki Theodoracopulos

Many Americans derive a great deal of comfort from the idea that there will always be an England, and consequently English things—from *Masterpiece Theatre* to Barbara Pym novels to a distinctive style of English décor. The latter flourishes in the decorating work of New York designer Mario Buatta, the so-called "Prince of Chintz."

One of Buatta's stylish Englishing projects was the transformation of an American city brownstone into a nineteenth-century English town house at the request of the writer Taki Theodoracopulos and his family.

The basic four-story structure lent itself easily to Anglicization (or, as the decorator has been known to joke, "Buattification.") Buatta was given a head start by the architectural details in the house, including the twelve-foot ceilings, tall windows, Ionic columns and pilasters in the hallways and rooms, sculptured cornices, and arched bookcase niches. The furnishings were chosen in compliance with an unwritten English decorating dictum—coziness and comfort come from the mixture of periods and patterns.

Favored antique furnishings that were found during several of Buatta's and the Theodoracopuloses' shopping trips include a Chinese-style cabinet and rococo benches and several needlepoint rugs. Additional pieces

Preceding pages and above: *The cozy library perfectly illustrates the English use of pattern and different styles of furniture. Upholstered pieces, designed by Mario Buatta, and walls are in Georgian Scroll chintz by J.H. Thorp. Opposite: Library's leaded-glass bay window looks out to the rear of the house.*

were designed by Buatta and covered in an array of English prints and patterns.

Each room has the European owners' "English-casual-relaxed" requirement, but perhaps none more than the library, which, as might be expected in a writer's household, is the family's favorite. "We covered the entire room in the same fabric so the off-center window doesn't suddenly jump out at you," Buatta says, "and having the pattern all around makes it very cozy." (Perhaps the room's coziest touch is an often-used bay-window seat.) In the living room, where three windows insured plenty of sunlight, Buatta added yellow walls and curtains to "keep the sun in twenty-four hours a day."

In this way, Mario Buatta continues to encourage American application of the much-loved British sense of domestic style.

Roderick Cameron
for Anne Cox Chambers

In the sitting room and elsewhere, says Mrs. Chambers, "more people notice the painted floors than anything else." Armchair is English Regency. An 18th-century Chinese painting hangs over sofa with throw pillows in Fortuny fabric, also made up as table cover.

Not long after World War II a very large man began to push the doors of antiques shops all over Europe, but above all in London and Paris. Where known, he was greeted with unfeigned pleasure. Where not known, he was quickly appreciated for the speed of his eye, his breadth of knowledge, and his powers of decision. He did not come every day, or every week, or every month, but when he did come he went unerringly to what he most wanted and began to take it in through long straight fingers. Touch and texture were almost as important to him as sight.

Though born an American citizen, Roderick Cameron was of mingled Scottish and Australian descent. Travel was always an important part of his life, and ever since he was taken into the tomb of King Tutankhamen not long after it was discovered he had a passion for places in which exceptional events had taken place or in which there were natural resources of a kind to be found nowhere else. (His first published work was an essay on the Great Barrier Reef, off the coast of Australia, that appeared in *Horizon* magazine in England, when Cyril Connolly was its editor.)

Later, and as one decade followed another, it became known that he had made for himself one house

The Charles Lees
painting of Drummond
Castle in the living room
was chosen by Rory
Cameron as "very restful,
to set the tone of the
room." Coffee table
displays a 19th-century
French bronze
greyhound. On table at
left is a rare Tibetan
crystal mask. Queen
Anne stools—"Rory was
particularly keen about
them"—wear
contemporary
needlepoint; chair fabric
from Tassinari & Chatel
in Paris. End tables
covered in fabric by
John Stefanidis.

after another which had classic status. There was a very large one called La Fiorentina, on St-Jean-Cap-Ferrat (in the south of France), and a rather smaller one nearby, called Le Clos. (During the period of transition between these two there was a house that was really very small indeed called Humble Pie.) There was also a house in Donegal, in Ireland, and when the French Riviera got altogether too much for him he moved inland to Ménerbes, near Avignon, where he made a house and garden called Les Quatres Sources.

That might have been the end of it, as far as he was concerned, if he had not made friends with a neighbor in Provence who lived in Atlanta but was buying an apartment on the East Side of Manhattan. The Honorable Anne Cox Chambers, who had been United States Ambassador to Belgium during the Carter Administration, was immediately interested and intrigued by the phenomenon of Rory Cameron.

Here was someone who never seemed to be busy, never ran after anything or anyone, and never collected for collecting's sake. In company he was benignity itself, and never put himself forward. Only after long acquaintance did one find out that he had published pioneering studies of Kenya, India, the South Seas, Latin America, and Australia. By instinct, rather than by book learning, he was one of the last of the all-rounded connoisseurs, as much at home with the study of a moth whose wings span ten inches as with the pale carved topazes that he had brought back from Sri Lanka and the fragments of Roman glass that he had brought back from North Africa.

Unlike scholars who "know everything" but cannot conjugate their knowledge with the business of living, Rory Cameron had an infallible sense of what to do with a house. To mix and mate one object with another was both his genius and his greatest pleasure. Better than almost anyone around, he knew how to release the conviviality of objects. The same applied to his sense of architecture—for the cut of a staircase, the proportions of a column, or the precise span of an arcaded arch.

What could be more natural than that Anne Cox Chambers should seek to enlist her remarkable neighbor as adviser when the time came to move into her New York apartment? And what could be more natural than that he, who so much loved shopping and had no new house of his own to work on, should say yes? What followed was a whirlwind shopping spree (two or three days in London, one or two in Paris) in which nothing was bought without good reason but all well-founded whims could be indulged. She loved it. He loved it. What situation could be more ideal?

It was fundamental to the adventure that he was to get *everything* from beginning to end—furniture, objects, china, knives and forks, glasses, tablecloths, curtains, carpets, pictures. He had a completely free hand. If he felt like having the floors painted—something he had never done before—it was done. If he had an instinct for

Left: *Chairs at English Regency dining table are 18th-century giltwood. Amusing paintings are Flemish interpretations of engravings made in China by a Jesuit priest.*
Below left: *Vertès screen by bed was the only element Mrs. Chambers owned before Rory Cameron started putting the apartment together. English 18th-century bergère in Zumsteg fabric; Regency lacquer bench; 19th-century English glass and lacquer cabinet; painted Italian commode. Bed hangings, Clarence House.*
Opposite: *In the living room, an 18th-century Chinese rug on raffia matting. Italian cartouche, Korean faience deer, English giltwood armchair are 18th century as well.*

one particular cushion in a shop piled high with them, they went in and got it. If there was a Chinese silk carpet that looked too small for the apartment, he laid it on plain raffia (from Cogolin in the south of France) and it looked just right.

It was also fundamental to the adventure that Mrs. Chambers should get to go along on the hunt. In this way she got what used to be called "a liberal education." But it was not an education of a preachy, cut-and-dried kind. Rory Cameron worked for a quality of repose. Bustle and confusion and untidiness were not for him. But neither was he in the least a doctrinaire aesthete who worked to rule. He never said to Mrs. Chambers, "Buy this" or "Buy that." He simply said, "Do think about that a bit. It's such a treasure." (Once or twice she said, "That's too grand for me," and he said, "That's nonsense," but in general he chose what he would most like for himself and she was delighted to go along with it.) "He was *never* pushy," is what she most remembers from their trips together. Except for a screen by Vertès in her bedroom, everything in the apartment was chosen by Rory Cameron, and with her. He rarely overspent, either, even if there was a code word of his—"*vast*," for the price of an object—that alerted her to the possibility of a rather large bill. "Not *vast*" was also a favorite expression of his, and she heard it more often than not.

It was a novelty for her, and one that was—if one may so put it—*vastly* amusing. As they padded from shop to shop, she observed that there was something almost disconcerting about the speed with which Rory Cameron crossed the desiderata off his very long list. His eye for size, shape, and predestined location was unerring. (Years ago when planning for his own house in Ireland he selected piece after piece almost without bothering to measure them, only to find on arrival in Donegal that every one of them fitted snugly into the space that he had in mind for them.)

Rory Cameron died before the apartment was quite finished, but going around it is like a last conversation with him—and a last review of his idiosyncratic and completely unprejudiced tastes. If he found a ninth-century Tibetan crystal mask, he had it sent. If Fortuny cottons seemed to him right for a draped table and some pillows, he had them made up. If Mrs. Chambers wanted a table setting that would do for impromptu spaghetti suppers with her children, he did not demur but went off to Bloomingdale's, where the salespeople ate out of his hand and he treated the job as seriously as if he had been in Spink's or

Mallett's in London, not to mention their often uppity counterparts in Paris.

"Everything he chose worked out, except once. He ordered two commodes from a man he knew in Paris—we couldn't find old ones with the right dimensions. It took forever—Rory thought he'd sold them without telling us—and then when at last they came, he took one look at them and said, 'They're too big. I made a mistake. They're that much too long,' and I said that we'd look at them for a while and see if we came around to them. But next morning when I came down, very early, he was already downstairs looking very distraught and said, 'They won't do at all. They'll be fine in Atlanta, but here they're not right at all.' So I said, 'If that's your only mistake—why, that's wonderful.' "

And it was Rory Cameron's only mistake, and the apartment was—and is—wonderful, and a tribute both to a discerning patron and to a most gifted man.

Jack Ceglic for Joel Dean

*I*n the world of chanterelle mushrooms and herbed goat cheese, Joel Dean is a folk hero, if yuppies can be called folk. His Dean & DeLuca food and housewares market in Manhattan's SoHo helped gentrify that once-crumbling neighborhood and established a merchandising and display style—crowded Victorian food hall built from high-tech components—that is still being cloned by competitors. Then Dean & DeLuca cloned itself in a second store in East Hampton, and Joel Dean decided to establish a Long Island pied-à-terre.

He asked an old friend and business associate, Jack Ceglic, to help him find and decorate a house. Ceglic began his professional life as an artist, but a second talent emerged when he designed the SoHo Dean & DeLuca in 1977. He has since designed other stores, several residences, and the faculty club at Columbia University's College of Physicians and Surgeons. What interests Jack Ceglic is "molding spaces," whether it means breaking up large areas into manageable units or making small rooms seem unconfining.

The Joel Dean cottage, which adds up to just 20 by 27 feet of downstairs living space under a half-story bedroom, gave Jack Ceglic a chance to make the most of minimal square footage. The 1927 house was so dilapidated when the men first saw it that other potential buyers had

The deep backyard was one of the reasons this tiny cottage in East Hampton, Long Island, was bought. To the right thrives a wide, three-season border; an existing arbor was retained.

Four views of the compact (20 by 27 feet) downstairs living space. Wildflowers and choice objects find it a perfect setting and with books supply most of the color. Window "curtains" of pleated butcher paper on wooden dowels last about two years. Jack Ceglic painting and drawings.

turned right around. (A neighbor says she was able to buy her house at a bargain price "because of the wreck next door.") Dean and Ceglic recognized the handsome proportions and the remnants of original details; also, the cottage was just the right size to be an easily maintained, no-guests retreat for a single man with a hectic job—as weekend party time approaches and the last of the green-peppercorn pâté and chocolate mousse cake has been snapped up, the tension in the store spreads like a stock-market panic. Afterward Joel Dean likes to go home and read. Jack Ceglic says, "I designed a house where he could read in every room and several parts of the garden."

Jack Ceglic's description of what he did sounds simple: "I took it all apart and remade it as it originally was." But the job was not nearly as simple as it might have been. Every surface, inside and outside, was meticulously executed. The wall paint, for example, is a warm white where the north light hits it and cool white under the light from the south; the window trim is pale buff and the door trim is pale gray—"to relieve the eye, to give an illusion of space and movement," says Ceglic. "No one actually notices the differences."

The downstairs is essentially two rooms: a kitchen-dining room and a living room. The black-and-white Kentile floor, similar to a scrap of flooring found there, flows throughout. A new stainless steel restaurant-chef's counter runs the length of the kitchen's longest wall, but the old twenties gas stove remains. Joel Dean finds it more sensitively calibrated than any new one, and besides, Jack Ceglic was fond of the stove as "a symbol of cooking." Symbols of home life are as important in his decorating as symbols of food and equipment are in the stores.

The dining furniture, designed by De Stijl architect J.J.P. Oud and reproduced now by Ecart, typifies the taste for early-twentieth-century design that Dean and Ceglic share. In the narrow living room, which had been two tiny rooms before, comfortable muslin-clad sofas mirror each other, and a Carlos Riart rocker from Knoll International faces a Scandinavian wood stove that can heat the entire house. An enclosed front porch flanks this room, and with the original front window removed and side slot windows added, it functions as a barrier against street sounds and flashing car lights. It is yet another thoughtful feature of a house designed to read in, quietly.

Antony Childs
for Ramon Osuna

Washington, D.C., is a city of lived-in American history. Every house is a bit of an archaeological dig. But in 1978 an actual street became a collector's item, when a certain stretch of Sixteenth Street, rehabilitated after a deep mid-twentieth-century decline, was designated historic. That was also when art dealer and collector Ramon Osuna bought his 1890 stone-and-brick house.

A native of Cuba, Osuna has known Washington since childhood; diplomacy and politics are in his blood. He first left Havana at age seven when Eleanor Roosevelt recommended he attend The Landon School in Maryland. After that it was a life of travel following his father's diplomatic career (the elder Osuna was at the Cuban Embassy in Washington for thirty years). From ages thirteen through sixteen, Osuna was taught by tutors on the road. A natural subject was art, for collecting in the family had begun with his paternal great-grandfather. Osuna bought his own first picture, a Cuban primitive portrait, at the age of sixteen.

Osuna's college career in Havana coincided with the first two years of Fidel Castro's revolution. During this time he helped reorganize the Havana Museum, putting on a major exhibition of Cuban painters at Villanova University. But 22 months after the revolution Osuna-family properties were confiscated, and on September 14, 1960, Osuna left Cuba for Washington for the last time.

For nine years in Washington Osuna worked in the Visual Arts Department of The Organiza-

tion of American States and helped make about fifteen documentaries on Latin American art with narrators like Jose Ferrer. As for American art, Osuna had begun to collect work by the Washington-based artists Ed McGowin, Lowell Nesbitt, and Gene Davis, among others—"Washington was ahead of New York then in the Pop and Color Field movements"—as well as the Baroque art he'd been surrounded by as a child. Soon he decided to open a gallery.

With partner Luis Lastra, who had been a friend in Havana and had also worked at the O.A.S., Osuna opened the Pyramid Gallery on January 25, 1970. The show was called a "beauty" by the critic Ben Forgey, a mixture of "styles, nationalities, and generations that one might erroneously assume would not mix in any harmonious way. Yet there it all is on the walls...looking like an exceptional, very personal, private collection." This has remained the Osuna format at home and in his gallery.

In the late seventies Osuna, without Lastra, relocated downtown, spearheading the move to bring galleries nearer the capital's art museums. But this new gallery was to be for contemporary art alone. Because "older paintings can't be stored, handled, and as easily shown as contemporary paintings in racks," Osuna decided to show the seventeenth through nineteenth centuries in his house on Sixteenth Street.

Combining the personal with the professional in Osuna's house was a project for which Osuna called upon Antony Childs, an interior designer who is known for work that is elegant and formal but not forbidding. Such was his approach with Osuna's historic house. Furnished with Regency pieces and Osuna's Empire collection (upholstered in contemporary striped cotton), the house is hung with Baroque-era European and Spanish masters and lit by an art gallery's flexible system of washes and spots to bring any and all aspects of the interior into focus. Most of the doors in the house were removed so that the ten rooms can provide unobtrusive wall space for a possible sixty paintings. Four stories give adequate floor space for fifteen sculptures. But despite the collections, the milieu Childs has helped Osuna create is uncluttered. This is a house "devoted to having paintings on the walls," says the owner, who prefers to change them often. With every painting on brass chains, the house could be sold out and rehung from top to bottom in eight hours.

It is in the dining and living rooms on the second floor that Osuna's and Childs's idea of home and gallery best succeed. Entrance archways to these two

Above: *A bust of the young George Washington dominates the street side of the third-floor sitting room. Striped linen is by Henry Calvin.* Right: *A Baltimore Empire secretary looms beside two dainty Austrian oils. In the hall,* The Beheading of St. John the Baptist *by the 18th-century Neapolitan artist Paolo di Matteis. Sofa and ottoman fabric by Glant.*

Above: *In the dining room a Susquehanna River landscape by Paul Weber hangs above a mantelpiece thought to be from the U.S. Grant White House. Busts by Hiram Powers. At room's end,* The Battle of Alameck *by Jean Léon Gérôme. Dining table by Jeffrey Bigelow.* Right: *Painting over bar in the sitting room is Emmanuel Michel Benner's* Hercules Between Virtue and Vice, 1899. *Throw pillows, Decorators Walk.*

Above: *A bust of Daniel Webster stays in the guest bedroom, between American Empire bed and sofa. Reclining girl is by William Oliver, a 19th-century English painter. Brunschwig strié wallpaper.* Opposite: *An* Architectural Fantasy *by a Neapolitan follower of Viviano Codazzi sets the tones of the master bedroom. Bust looking over the American Empire bed is by Richard Saltonstall Greenough. Cotton duck by Westgate.*

rooms show that Childs has been inspired by the neoclassical architect Sir John Soane (1753–1837). Instead of mirroring the book niches, Childs mirrored the tops and sides of both entrances to lighten thick nineteenth-century walls, "give a sense of fantasy, see the paintings from another perspective."

Ramon Osuna's life involves frequent entertaining. His house hosts probably the only four-story dinners in the nation's capital. As many as 75 guests at a time stroll its stairwells, make themselves comfortable in its rooms, and eat *pastelón,* a sweet Cuban chicken pie with plums. Both Osuna and Childs insist this is a nighttime house. Lit for evening as you come up its front walk (even the skylight has artificial lighting), the house shines bright daylight from every window.

What a visitor sees first behind the wrought-iron, glass-front doors is Mlle. Befort's *Theban Soldier Consoled by Daughter.* The daughter's brilliant tomato-red dress is ineffably classic, of another time and place. The spotlight is so subtle on the fall of the skirt, it is hard to tell whether the light is electric or candle and whether the century is the twentieth or the nineteenth, when the Osuna house was brand-new.

Denning & Fourcade for Oscar de la Renta

*O*scar de la Renta has come to regard his apartment as something of a retreat where he can escape the consequences of being so much in demand. But when he and his late wife, Françoise, first moved in, these romantic rooms were primarily conceived for entertaining. Even now the notion of them bereft of guests is anomalous. So when we look at the photographs on these pages we have to imagine that it is not daytime but eight-thirty of an early winter evening, and guests are on their way up for one of Oscar's memorable dinners. The imperturbable James—formerly a footman at Buckingham Palace—has just lit the candles and put the last touches to the grog tray. The heat from the wood fire is opening up hundreds of parrot tulips jammed into urn after urn. And the host, no doubt, is casting an eagle eye on things in the kitchen, before emerging to welcome his guests.

"Our rooms are to give the impression that they evolved over the generations, never touched by a decorator," say Robert Denning and Vincent Fourcade, who are responsible for executing the de la Renta apartment to exactly that effect. The partnership they formed in 1960 was based on their lavish interpretation of the late-nineteenth-century style, and except for a certain loosening up, they have held to that style and watched the rest of the design

Above: A Royal German Family Traveling in Egypt, 1846, *by Johann Hermann Kretschmer hangs over the sofa covered in antique printed Victorian plush. In foreground, a bronze by Gianbologna and a pair of 19th-century columns after the Colonne Vendôme.* Opposite: *In another corner of the living room, divided by columns found by Vincent Fourcade, an 18th-century mirror with blue glass hangs over the faux bois fireplace.*

world catch up. As steadfast as the partnership and the style is the friendship of their clients. They are probably expected for dinner tonight.

In they flock, guests full of anticipation, knowing that unlike most of the New York dinners they are obliged to attend, this one is bound to be amusing, and mercifully free of business, for Oscar makes a point of leaving business behind at his office. Instead of hours wasted drinking before dinner, there is just enough time for people to touch base, above all with new arrivals from Paris or London or the host's native Santo Domingo. Outside the windows of Oscar's living room the lights in Central Park form mysterious constellations; inside the flicker of candles highlights the glint of ormolu, the gleam of marble and bronze. The mirages that materialize on the walls turn out to be the host's collection of Orientalist paintings—odalisques

primping, camels ruminating, Bedouin hordes reconnoiter-
ing an oasis, and—best of all—Johann Hermann Kretz-
schmer's spectacular group of a Prussian prince inspect-
ing Saharan loot for his trophy room at Schloss Berlin. But
besides setting off Oscar's Benjamin Constants, Ernsts, and
Fromentins, the deep garnet glow of the walls provides
the perfect foil for jeweled women in jewel-colored dresses—dresses shimmering with paillettes that Oscar employs
with Bakst-like abandon. And how painterly people look in
this setting. A stark avian profile against the black and gold
of a Boulle bookcase recalls Sargent's *Madame X.,* while
across the room, a group of French ladies in tulle and dia-
monds conjures up Winterhalter.

      The dining room, whither Oscar's guests
proceed with a great silken rustle, is no less nineteenth century in feeling than the living room. However, we no longer
seem to be in France, but somewhere farther east. The paneling simulates *bois clair* inlaid with ebony and the blue-and-
white pots either side of the window are big enough to
conceal a couple of mamelukes. The effect is nothing if not
festive—all the more so for Oscar's impressive collection of
eighteenth-century English silver, floral porcelain, and en-
graved glass—but for many of these habitués the dining
room evokes sad memories of the late Françoise de la Renta.
For it was above all here, in the dining room, that the legendary hostess reached her apogée as *the* New York catalyst;
here that, for the fifteen years or so before her untimely
death in 1983, she established a benign sway over some of
the most gifted and attractive, not to say powerful, people to
be found at any one time in the city—people of all ages, nationalities, professions, and degrees. Granted, many were
social stars, but many more were simply friends.

A Regency mirror with crocodiles hangs over two Russian hurricane lamps on 19th-century library table in front hall; between them is a terra cotta by Clodion (a project for a fountain) and a Roman marble. Empire chairs in the Egyptian style are on either side.

Left: *The bedroom,
divided from the dressing
room by velvet portières,
has a Viennese bed
surrounded by icons,
19th-century landscapes.*
Below left: *Sitting room,
like bedroom, has walls
in Lee Jofa fabric.*
Opposite: *Dining room
cabinet designed by
Fourcade displays
Chinese porcelain.*

For those who fondly called Françoise "*La Générale*" life will never run as smoothly as it did under her auspices. Yet posthumously she continues to be a source of inspiration, not least to her husband, who goes from strength to strength in large part by living up to her formidable standards. In the aftermath of Françoise's death, Oscar devoted much of his time to planning a magnificent garden in Connecticut—all avenues and borders—in her memory. The New York apartment is also a memorial to her taste. Apart from adapting it to bachelorhood, Oscar required from Denning & Fourcade no major changes to the overall look. Their principal transformation was knocking the library and living room into one so as to create more space. Space for what? "Entertaining, I suppose," Oscar replies with his sheepish grin. But he also cherishes his privacy and has had his bedroom, which is tucked away behind velvet portières and French doors turned from a study and dressing room, into a quiet refuge.

Although Oscar makes a great point of keeping his professional life separate from his private life, this apartment constitutes a link between the two, in that the designer's eye for the romantic in décor tends to reflect the designer's eye for the romantic in clothes. Witness his passion for the opera. In the country the voice of Elisabeth Schwarzkopf singing Viennese operetta rings out over his spread in the Connecticut highlands; in New York the designer's taste turns more to Verdi. It is no coincidence that Oscar's living room, with its banquettes and *dos-à-dos* sofas, its passementerie and Austrian blinds, would make a perfect setting for *La Traviata*. Only here there is more refinement and sophistication and Oscar's guests are, for the most part, more respectable than Violetta's.

Bruce Gregga for Betsy and Andrew Rosenfield

Opposite above:
*Deborah Butterfield's
horses pasture in the
dining room of the
Rosenfields' Chicago
apartment. Buffet table at
left displays Dale
Chihuly's glass, a William
Morris vase; dining
table topped by Tom
Rippon's weight lifters.*
Opposite below: *In
bedroom, a Joseph
Piccillo horse, David
Sharpe screen, Bugatti
desk and chair.*

*A*ndrew and Betsy Rosenfield both started collecting in their early twenties. She is the daughter of art collectors, as well as an active member of Chicago's Museum of Contemporary Art, proprietor of her own art gallery, a former art history student, and collector of orchids and tiny wind-up toys. He is a patron of the Art Institute of Chicago with a penchant for collecting everything from turntables and books to early-twentieth-century European furniture.

What they wanted when they acquired this sprawling 1930s apartment was space to house an enviable and exuberant collection in a setting that would be both visually effervescent and livable for them and their son. A collaborative effort by Chicago-based interior designer Bruce Gregga and architect Marvin Herman, the project relies on such fundamental underpinnings as a carefully plotted restoration of the apartment's vintage trimmings and the application of new but compatible detailing.

"It was mostly a matter of correlating the architecture with the furnishings and the art," Gregga modestly notes. "The fringe benefit was being able to use the furniture collection as art. We worked together, respecting the old and adding things that would fit with the Rosenfields' way of life." That life revolves around a continuing

This Josef Hoffmann grouping fired the couple's furniture-collecting passion. Sculpture by William Carlson.

Top: *The den, which is occupied by the paintings of Roger Brown, Jedd Garet, and Mark Jackson.* Above: *Dan Dailey's blue glass vase, Lucas Samaras's wire sculpture, and a pair of Ed Paschke paintings flanking the door to the den.*

quest for high-quality works of art in a variety of media—from the razzle-dazzle paintings of Chicagoans Ed Paschke and Roger Brown to the whimsy of a Botero drawing or the brilliance of glass art by Dale Chihuly and William Carlson.

"We started collecting Chicago 'Imagists,' then came the furniture, then the glass, then the sculpture, then New York artists," say the Rosenfields. "We don't collect for investment. We collect what we like—art that works for us visually more than conceptually.

"The furniture represents the first statement of modernity and is beautifully simple, not intricately adorned but superbly crafted. We care about that. We don't want something that's 'here today and gone tomorrow.' And, too, there's only so much room for paintings."

While the couple edited the collection, Gregga laid it out, bringing order to the diverse array of paintings, furniture, and sculpture and tempering the display with a gentle hand to ensure a welcoming environment that heightens the impact of the pieces.

"When we first saw the apartment, there was a fountain in the foyer," explains Gregga, who quickly devised a plan for removal of the fixture and for some reworking of the walls in the entry area to maximize display space. Doors to closets and a powder room were ripped out and traffic rerouted. Floors were refinished and new millwork that replicates the old—primarily molding—was installed where molding had never been. Now the moldings visually frame every space in what was conceived as a virtually blank canvas for the installation of the collection.

The catch, of course, was how to make the live-in gallery—complete with humidity controls—read like a residence rather than a series of unrelated displays. In that interest, Gregga and Herman shunned the use of such gallery bugaboos as track lighting and chalk-white walls. An almost invisible system, the lighting throughout the apart-

In the entry Michael Stevens's Chinaman's Chance *faces Mackintosh chairs and Don Baum's tiny house. Over the table: Mark Jackson's portraits of the owners. Jud Fine's four poles stand by Marisol's three people.*

Top: *A French Art Deco rug anchors the seating area dominated by the Bauer sofa and club chairs. To right of doorway, Roger Brown's "Murphy bed."* Above: *Ornate Bugatti desk in bedroom, further adorned by David Beck's box.*

Opposite: *In library, John Obuck's painting behind a Süe et Mar kingwood desk and a Hoffmann chair. Elephant box construction by Robert Bergman.*

ment consists of recessed downlights, wall washers, and framing spots. There is nary a lamp in sight, except for a task light or two, including a sleek Italian one on the desk in the study and a pair of early Richard Sapper bedside table lamps that predate his famous Tizio design. All this illumination plays off a restrained palette that intertwines painted blush-pink and lacquered aubergine walls. In the dining room, walls above the pale-pink wainscoting are upholstered in a heavily textured, glazed pine-green fabric that at first glance looks like leather.

"The colors simultaneously complement and subdue the power of the art," notes Gregga. "This project was not at all a matter of bashing down entire walls. A lot of what we did is unseen in a sense, but the place really has a very nice feeling."

Gregga grouped Josef Hoffmann tables and a trio of Leopold Bauer seating pieces on top of a French Deco area rug to reinforce the sense of intimacy suggested by the color scheme. And he scrupulously avoided positioning things around the perimeters of rooms. Both the bedroom and study desks were placed to cut the corners of the rooms. The dining room contains a pair of carefully unmatched tables—a dark, angular design with a boxy base and a skirted-to-the-floor round one. When not put into service as a dinner-party buffet, the dark table is the stage for a changing array of art glass and small sculpture.

Throughout the apartment the subdued furniture and bold art have a symbiotic relationship. Michael Stevens's chairlike *Chinaman's Chance* in the entry hall, for example, is a delightful counterpoint to the room's pair of Mackintosh chairs.

"The real joy of the apartment," say the Rosenfields, "is that it's always changing, things are being moved around and maneuvered. That's the adventure and that's what makes it home. We're far from 'done.'"

Architect Yann Weymouth's unadorned table and Mark Hampton's simple couch are foils for Ashton Hawkins's real furnishings—his art collection. Bob Smith's Camel Train *above couch makes witty reference to The Metropolitan Museum of Art's King Tut show, which Hawkins helped arrange.*

Mark Hampton
for Ashton Hawkins

Ashton Hawkins is general counsel for The Metropolitan Museum of Art. He is also secretary of the museum's board of trustees and all the board's committees. He is also one of the museum's six vice-presidents.

The constant switching of administrative hats leaves Ashton Hawkins precious little time for the casual lunch, the afternoon vacation, or even a random walk through the museum. Nor does it allow him to stumble home after work and recharge. On the contrary: night after night he is expected to represent the museum's interests in the dining and drawing rooms of New York's Upper East Side. Small wonder that when he finally gets home, he does not choose to find himself in a space that reminds him either of the museum or Park Avenue.

Still, it is something of a surprise to walk into Ashton Hawkins's apartment ten floors above Central Park West and see how little it resembles the double-breasted public persona of its owner. The ceiling is appropriately high and the moldings are traditionally dark, but the walls are covered with a collection of modern art and photography so eclectic that even a curator at the Whitney would be shocked at their variety. And the space bears so little rela-

Left: *View from dining room suggests an apartment of baronial proportions, a trick made possible by framing effect of columns.* Above: *David Hockney's 1978* Pool with Cloud Reflections *hangs over Yann Weymouth's table of black lacquer and polished steel.*

tionship to the gloomy and chopped-up warrens that were once the hallmark of Central Park West that, for a minute, you could think you're in a downtown loft.

And those are just the introductory surprises. After you've negotiated the generous foyer and the picture-crammed gallery, you find yourself in a 33-by-20-foot living-dining room that suggests vast space beyond. A parlor beckons through double doors. Enter it, though, and you'll find yourself in the 10-by-12 bedroom. Here, unless your curiosity extends to Hawkins's Gatsbyesque shelves of shirts, your tour has ended.

This sense of disproportion—"Turn a corner and you're there," says Hawkins's friend Mark Hamp-

Top: *Four hand-colored lithographs by David Roberts hang above Hawkins's bed/sofa.* Above: *A ceramic model of the Plaza Hotel and a 1981 sculpture by Tom Otterness do not obstruct bedroom's view of a church, the Museum of Natural History, and the Beresford apartments.*

ton—and a mazelike layout with two foyers and three hallways were the main design features of the apartment when Hawkins bought it. The lack of access made the apartment, as Hawkins notes with lawyerly understatement, "less expensive than it might have been." It also suggested that any renovation would have to be so complete that the idea of economy should be instantly discarded. Architect Yann Weymouth, an old friend, at first thought the apartment should be a series of rooms in the spirit of the lobby of the 1907 building (the only feature he liked), but then he recalled that Hawkins tended to give informal, sprawling parties that might go off better in a loftlike space. In the end, the owner and architect agreed on a compromise plan, which Hawkins calls "a postmodern space with overtones of the Edwardian period." The renovation took six months.

Enter—or rather, reenter—Mark Hampton. Not only had Hampton designed Hawkins's former apartment, he and his wife, Duane, were, with Hawkins, founding members of what may be the longest-running reading group in New York. The dozen members of this group plow through one novelist a year, meeting once every month for lunch or dinner on Sundays. Though their conversation is free-form, the ground rules are not: members may not read biographies or secondary sources until the end of the year, and no one may attend who hasn't read the book under discussion. Though Hawkins has been lobbying unsuccessfully for Mark Twain for a good part of the last decade, he is still—after a dozen years—the group's most enthusiastic member.

So Mark Hampton wasn't just designing an apartment—he was designing rooms he intended to sit in. For that reason, there was some creative tension between architect and designer. "Yann's plan was compounded by the collage scrapbook quality Ashton brings to his life," Hampton explains. "He has a wonderful liveliness that makes him continually change things. My job was to anchor the rooms down so there'd be some predictability."

What is most impressive about Hampton's work is how few anchors he needed. He deaccessioned some of the furniture he'd chosen for Hawkins in the past, built two mahogany panels for more privacy in the bedroom, and created a zebra-skin screen to replace a zebra rug that had become a cliché. Then he wisely got out of the way and let the collector fill the room with his art, which Hawkins calls "the real furnishings of the apartment."

This art ranges from the personally priceless to the actually valuable—with no space separating the extremes. In the foyer, for openers, a Robert Murray sculpture

American desk and chair against the far wall in the bedroom are circa 1840. Mahogany screens were designed by Mark Hampton. Bed/sofa is covered in a woven jute fabric by Brunschwig & Fils, with kilim pillows.

overlooks a basket of egg-shaped granite rocks that Hawkins finds himself inexplicably carting home from each visit to the Maine coast. A picture of his Russian-born mother sits across from a picture of his great friend the writer Renata Adler and next to the lid of a nineteenth-century Russian box that Hawkins found in London and had framed. And along the back wall of the foyer, near what Hawkins describes as "the wine and art closet," are a nineteenth-century watercolor of Lake George and an Yvonne Jaquette pastel of the view from her studio on a rainy night.

The hallway is just as varied. Avedon, Mapplethorpe, and Penn fight for attention with an anonymous turn-of-the-century Indian photographer. One of the seven etchings made by Barnett Newman hangs near a mezzotint by Claes Oldenburg and an Ed Ruscha with the word "Ash" in smoke writing. And a turn into the guest bath brings a stunning view of half a blue sailfish mounted over the tub.

A Frankenthaler set on a Regency stand, a Noland, several early works by Albers—can be found in the living room, but they're given no more prominence than a piece of bent and etched glass by Christopher Wilmarth and a Navaho chief's blanket Hawkins's father bought in Santa Fe in the twenties. Near the bookshelves filled with complete sets of authors his reading group has tackled, he has filled display cases with "memorabilia and oddities" that most other collectors would consign to a drawer. And stationed on a window sill in this room is a T'ang camel—"everybody's favorite exotic animal"—and a stuffed bear from a dinner on the theme of *Brideshead Revisited*.

All this art may, from time to time, be loaned to museums or stored to make room for new purchases. Two small works, though, are certain to remain on permanent exhibition. Both have, as they say, some history. One is the first painting Hawkins bought, a landscape he found for five dollars when he was at Exeter. He had no artistic ability himself, there were no collectors in his family, and although he was planning to be a lawyer, he had no idea of working for an institution that would remunerate him with titles instead of worldlier rewards. Still, he says dryly, the acquisition of this picture was certainly a harbinger.

The other is a watercolor about the size of a postcard. It shows a woman lounging against a column and looking into a blue background. The title is printed below: *Marion Davies Standing by Ashton's Pool*. The artist? Mark Hampton. As a housewarming gift from a designer who's also a painter to a collector who's also a friend, it has a certain charm. Then one remembers that Mark Hampton was also, very briefly, a lawyer, and the resonance deepens.

Mac II
for Bill Blass

Wat is admirable about Bill Blass's sense of style is its sinew. There is no flab or flashiness or folderol about it—no nostalgia. Despite a passion for the art of the past, this designer has seldom sought inspiration outside his own country, his own experience, or his own time. Down-to-earth Yankee swagger has always been his trademark, with a touch of restraint that could be described as puritan.

This element of restraint is much in evidence in the penthouse apartment that Bill Blass, with his old friend Chessy Rayner of Mac II, redecorated for two excellent reasons. After twenty years as a tenant, he had been able to buy the place; he had also grown tired of the high-fashion décor—brown walls and lots of *objets*—that he had formerly espoused. However, Blass was in no mood for the needlepoint and chintz or buttoned velvet and expensive fringe that many of his friends had adopted. Besides knowing what he didn't want, Blass had an exact idea of what he did want: everything to be quietly comfortable, subdued in color. "Very spare settings for very good things—good bones," is how he described it.

The first step was a ruthless clearing out of virtually everything inside as well as outside the apartment, not least the picturesque planting on the huge terraces. Blass

A view through a mahogany-and-glass Louis XVI screen into the light-filled living room: on left, a magnificent trompe-l'oeil painting of muskets and standards by the 17th-century Dutch painter Jacobus Biltius hangs over a late-18th-century Irish side table between a pair of Georgian globes on mahogany bases.

had the courage to rid himself of collections that had taken over thirty years to form: collections that included a few youthful follies but also many items—good Oriental things, for instance—that you and I would have given our eyeteeth for. Tabula rasa achieved, he asked Mac II to correct and simplify the architecture of the rooms.

The first correction, which the designers added to Blass's original plan, was to create a large gallery where a choppy entrance had been. Other major alterations included transforming a closet into a proper bath and streamlining the kitchen, in the process closing off its door into the living room. Stronger, more modern windows (the apartment is on the windy top floor) went into the bedroom, and the terrace was resurfaced in terra cotta.

Then it was time to paint all (except the hall's walls) what Blass described as "pale paper-bag color." The same neutral color was prescribed for the heavy but absolutely plain stuff for curtains and sofas. Where necessary, doors and bookcases were mahoganized. The only remotely

Above and opposite above: *In the living room, neutral sofas sit on a 19th-century Aubusson. To right of massive Charles II cabinet, an 18th-century trelliswork chair. Unusual polygonal late-18th-century mirror hangs over mantel, flanked by Oudry drawings of the fables of LaFontaine.* Opposite below: *An early-18th-century French trompe-l'oeil painting and a tapestry done after it depict a marble relief of Vulcan's forge.*

decorative feature was a purplish brown marble floor in the hall. It all took much longer than expected but Mac II had come up with exactly what was wanted: an elegant, modern background that draws little attention to itself.

While these transformations were under way, Blass went about forming a collection of old master drawings—a collection originally destined to cover the living room walls. In the end the scale of the room turned out to require things with "wall-power" (to quote a certain crass dealer), so most of the drawings have been hung in the bedroom. And surprisingly good they look massed together, these Oudrys and Menzels, Bibienas and Burne-Joneses, to name but a few of the artists represented in this heterogeneous collection. Meanwhile the living room has been hung with a collection of fine trompe-l'oeil paintings dating from the seventeenth and eighteenth centuries.

Details of the Blass style.
Top left: *An 18th-century marble lion atop mahogony secrétaire by Jean Henri Reisner.* Top right: *Georgian wine cooler beneath Irish side table.* Above: *Detail of bedroom secrétaire with* Fencing Master *by James Cammille Lignier, 1887.* Left: *Charles II cabinet veneered in oyster-spotted lignum vitae.* Right: *Stubbs over bedroom fireplace with leather-and-steel club fender.*

Top left: *A 19th-century watercolor of an interior on a late-18th-century Danish table with slate top.* Top right: *Pair of lions and photographs of dogs in front of old master drawings.* Above: *White roses in front of a study of parrot tulips attributed to 17th-century French painter Nicolas de Largillière.* Left: *Dressing room's open closets.* Right: *Stag legs of late-18th-century Swedish table.*

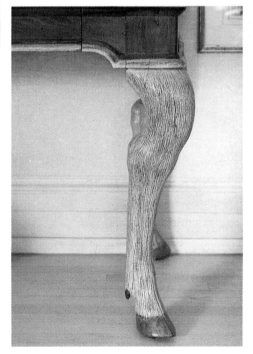

Left: *At far end of library/dining room, antique marble heads from Lord Pembroke's collection at Wilton sit on Italian fluted mahogany columns. Empire chairs covered in off-white sailcloth are Swedish. Brass library lights were copied from Charles de Beistegui's at Groussay. Library steps are 18th-century English. Below: In light-filled bedroom, two large obelisks sit on the windowsill, with terrace beyond. The walls have been hung with old master drawings including Bibiena, Barye, Landseer.*

The first major acquisition was a magnificent trompe-l'oeil painting (six feet by twelve feet) of muskets and standards stacked one above the other on racks. By the seventeenth-century Dutch painter Jacobus Biltius, it was acquired from Christopher Gibbs, the London dealer who specializes in the offbeat, the outsize, the magical. Gibbs was also the source for the superb Charles II cabinet, veneered in oyster-spotted lignum vitae, that dominates the north wall of the living room. This wood, with its flamboyant figuring, is rare enough in small pieces of furniture but virtually unheard of on this monumental scale. The only other lignum-vitae cabinet of this importance is in the Royal Collection at Hampton Court.

No less overscale is the heroic marble head that dominates the far end of the living room. When Blass first came upon this sculpture, it was covered in grime in the cellar of a London dealer. The head, which turned out to be by Marc Chabry (who worked with Pierre Puget, finest of French seventeenth-century sculptors), has cleaned up miraculously well. From the same dealer came the eighteenth-century terra-cotta torso by Innocenzo Spinazzi, which stands on one of the Italian Empire commodes either side of the fireplace. "Yes, I have developed a passion for sculpture," Blass admits, and he proposes to branch out further in this rewarding but still relatively unfashionable field.

The degree of Blass's reaction against pattern in decorating can be measured by comparing the way the dining room looks today with its former incarnation, when the walls and the furniture were covered in an extravagant Oriental chintz on a scarlet ground. Now the room has been transformed into a bright airy space that is as much a li-brary—one wall is devoted to the mahogany bookcases Mac II designed—as it is a dining room. Décor has once again been kept to a minimum: a set of Empire chairs that are probably Swedish, covered in off-white sailcloth; striking brass library lights like the ones that illuminated Charles de Beistegui's gigantic bookcases at Groussay; a pair of fluted mahogany columns (late-eighteenth-century Italian) crowned by antique marble heads from Lord Pembroke's celebrated collection at Wilton; and a rhapsodic oil sketch, attributed to Largillière, of parrot tulips scattered at random across a sepia ground.

With its paper-bag-colored walls and curtains, Blass's bedroom is of a piece with the living room. The only difference is that it is even more of a sanctum. There are stacks of books, and there are photographs of his great passion, Brutus and Kate, the golden retrievers that share his life in the country. Further signs of canine passion take the form of paintings and drawings of doggy subjects by artists such as Landseer and Albert Moore. However, the most important work of art in the bedroom is equine rather than canine: a magnificent painting of a bay horse in a landscape by George Stubbs. True, Blass, who has a penchant for a gamut of browns, enjoys the way the chestnut sheen of Stubbs's horse, fresh from the currycomb, picks up the mahogany sheen of Riesener's architectural desk standing next to it. But the affinity goes deeper than that. Stubbs's style and Blass's style have more in common than one might think. Although his gift as a designer has won him international fame, Blass remains an intensely private, country-lover at heart. This bay horse could not have found a more sympathetic or suitable owner.

Peter Marino
for Christopher Whittle

*P*eter Marino," Marie-Hélène de Rothschild was heard to reply when asked by a dinner companion to name the most sought-after architect/interior designer on the international axis. In this the age of nickel, Marino's penchant for time-tested luxury, indeed opulence, his unfailing attention to detail, his lavish use of wood paneling, hand stenciling, and gold and silver leafing, not to mention the stable of superb artisans he has cultivated to carry out his decorative designs, have attracted such clients as Marella and Giovanni Agnelli, Philippe Niarchos, Jacqueline de Ribes, Carla Fendi, Yves Saint Laurent, and Valentino.

"Appropriateness is the central point of architecture. A palace should look like a palace, a loft should look like a loft, and a hot-dog stand should look like a hot-dog stand," Marino states. "And an apartment in the Dakota should look like an apartment in the Dakota, not a sheikh's spread in the Olympic Tower," he adds pointedly, appraising what he accomplished for Christopher Whittle.

"I'd been living in a two-room log cabin just outside Knoxville, and the Dakota was the first apartment building I ever saw in New York—it spoiled me for other apartments," says Whittle, one of the two Tennessee whiz

In the living room, a Charles X clock sits on the Frank Furness fireplace under In a Rug Bazaar *by George Henry Hall. The English Regency table on left is from Gene Tyson and the 19th-century Sultanabad carpet from Doris Leslie Blau.*

kids who while still in college founded the 13–30 Group, a specialty-magazine publishing corporation, and went on to buy and resuscitate *Esquire* magazine. Today Whittle, while retaining the title of chairman of *Esquire,* where he is no longer active, is chairman and chief executive officer of Whittle Communications, which includes 21 media properties. To this son of an Etowah, Tennessee, country doctor and descendant of Ethan Allen of the Green Mountain Boys, the Dakota represented everything that Manhattan had to offer.

For Marino also, the pale-yellow-brick Victorian fortress on Central Park West at 72nd Street was the territory of his heart's desire. Constructed in 1884 by Henry Hardenbergh, who would later design the Plaza and old Waldorf-Astoria hotels in New York as well as the Copley Plaza in Boston and the Willard in Washington, the building was a triumph of splendid detail: carved marble mantels, elaborate stone friezes, arched and beamed floors three feet thick, paneled oak-and-mahogany walls. In the late 1960s the Dakota became a tourist attraction when Roman Polanski featured its exterior in *Rosemary's Baby;* its interior, however, was already the setting for film stars attracted to the drama of its dimensions and the privacy it afforded—everybody from Boris Karloff to Lauren Bacall has lived there.

The six-room apartment that Whittle purchased was so dilapidated he and Marino soon found themselves giving the lie to the following stanza of Marya Mannes's "Ballad of the Dakota":

> Oh, who of us would change a jot,
>> Or even an iota—
> We happy few whose happy lot
>> Is Life in the Dakota? . . .

"Not an inch of this flat—ceilings, walls, moldings, floors—was here when we started," Marino says, adding that a good renovation is sometimes the best preservation.

Marino's goal was to design the apartment as if Christopher Whittle were its very first resident, moving in in 1884. It therefore had to be reconstructed not only literally but by a feat of the imagination. It was—the apartment has a largess, a prodigality amounting to nothing less than an act of imaginative bestowal. Marino prides himself on being a dedicated historicist. "I would never do this apartment in any building *but* the Dakota," he says. "I researched the building's past, what the architect's point of view was, to achieve an authentic feeling."

For Marino, the project offered the additional opportunity to put together several period collec-

Lady on a Gold Couch,
circa 1906, by F.C.
Frieseke hangs over the
sofa. A large bronze of
Nathan Hale by
Frederick MacMonnies
rises on the right beyond
the goffered silk pillows;
the fabric on two of these
is 17th century. Imperial
Russian dessert plates set
the 19th-century table.

tions. "It was an A-to-Z job. Everything was collected especially for the apartment—right down to the Georgian silverware." Working with Whittle, for whom the apartment became a passionate preoccupation, Marino amassed an important collection of nineteenth-century European paintings, drawings, and watercolors and early-twentieth-century American paintings; a major pottery collection; even a collection of candlesticks, Russian, French Empire, Georgian cut crystal, American bronze, seventeenth-century English twirled wood, nineteenth-century English feldspar and jasper ("I wanted candlelight everywhere, fires in all the fireplaces, ormolu shimmering on the furniture. Look, the apartment was a dark hole. The essence of the Dakota is dark, of course, but it's Christopher Whittle's idea of merry—he's a very serious guy").

As in the nineteenth century, the major rooms are painted strong colors: the dining room oxblood, the living room gold, the study terra cotta. They were all done with pigment paints in the ultramatte nineteenth-century method where the colors were mixed with milk. Halls of the period were always neutral, so the central core of the Whittle apartment, a long windowless space called the gallery, is pale gray—decorated with stencils.

Dominating the gallery is a full-length portrait by the American Impressionist Richard Miller: a woman in a white shawl is looking into a mirror set above a commode. Marino found a large oval Regency mirror exactly like the one in the painting and hung it perpendicular to it, suggesting that it had been the artist's model. The twelve-foot-high gold-thread curtains on the portal from the gallery into the living room are from a set of late-nineteenth-century Aesthetic Movement curtains by Templeton of Glasgow that were in Wardour Castle in Wiltshire.

One of Marino's specialties is working directly with small factories in England, Italy, and France. The silk for the living room sofa was made in Lyon, and the sofa itself, designed by Marino after an 1880s model, was made by "a *tapissier* in Paris that's been in business for 140 years. And to make the curved steel frames for the upholstered chairs in the gallery, I used a company that's been making hoops for carriages for at least a century. I'm very proud of the workmanship I've been able to find."

French eighteenth-century decorative paintings of twelve Roman emperors in Renaissance garb reign supreme in the dining room—Nero, Octavianus, Claudius, Tiberius, Titus, Vespasian, Vitellius, Caligula, Galba, Otho, Domitian, and Julius Caesar. "When Peter first showed them to me," Whittle says, "I thought they were

In another view of the living room, two English 19th-century carved walnut chairs face each other to the left of a French Empire chair. The rosewood piano is circa 1870.

*In the dining room,
presided over by a large
Flemish chandelier,
griffins are the reigning
motif: on the firescreen,
Frank Furness mantel,
and Directoire carpet.
Over the fireplace hangs
a 1645 still life by Paulus
van den Bosch, between
twelve 18th-century
French paintings of
Roman emperors. A
crouching lion by
Antoine Louis Barye is
on the French 19th-
century table. Chairs
covered in Cowtan &
Tout silk damask are
George III.*

In the terra-cotta-colored guest room–study, Lady at a Writing Table, *circa 1890, by Julie Marest hangs to the left of pen-and-ink drawings of European street scenes by Lester Hornby. On the right is a French Empire desk and chair, across from a slipper chair in its original fabric, circa 1865.*

going to be the only modern thing in the apartment. When I heard eighteenth century, I was very surprised. Nineteen-twenties I would have guessed—they're kind of stylized."

Gustave Doré's monumental and brooding *Ruins by the Seacoast,* formerly in the Huntington Hartford collection, hangs on a side wall of the same room—a mood painting. The lofty fireplace is by the eminent American architect Frank Furness (Marino retrieved it from a Phila-delphia town house that was about to come down); griffins with feathery chests and ears are carved in the massive mahogany. There are also griffins etched in brass on the firescreen, and as the light flickers they appear to be mov-ing. In candlelight the whole ceiling scintillates, its thou-sands of hand-stenciled 22-carat-goldleaf triangles dissolv-ing the masculine solidity of the room. The walls wear a band under the cornice adapted from a Navaho blanket, then a second decorative border—above the wainscot pan-eling—from a housepainter's design book of the 1880s.

For Whittle the dining room has a double function. When he removes the eighteenth-century French silk-damask cloth from the French mahogany table, and opens hidden doors in the panel that reveal storage cabi-nets, telephones, and pads and pencils, he has an instant late-twentieth-century conference room.

In the 20-by-34-foot living room, "we start-ed with the carpet, as we always do in a major room," Marino says. It's a nineteenth-century Sultanabad—an Oriental garden carpet, deep blue with floating flowers. The Orientalist painting movement was one of the cross-currents of the time, and some of the flowers of that move-ment unfold on the living room walls. But the greatest painting in the room is the American Impressionist F. C. Frieseke's *Lady on a Gold Couch,* a richly patterned por-trait of the artist's wife reclining on a French settee, her head resting on ruffled pillows. It hangs above the sofa with its pillows of goffered silk.

The study/guest bedroom was a long shoe-box of a room, so Marino designed an alcove within it to make it appear less long, at the same time giving it an Orientalist look. He hung a pair of nineteenth-century Senneh kilim carpets, the same terra-cotta color as the room, on either side of the alcove and took stencil patterns from them for the walls and ceiling. Then he threw four Persian carpets on the floor, one on top of the other, and put a pair of rare Christofle vases, done in the 1880s in the Orientalist fashion with silver-and-copper inlays, on the fireplace. On the walls: a series of watercolors of flowering grasses, dated 1881. "They were used by Napoleon III's

Over the Northern Italian walnut bed, circa 1800, hangs a study for a painting of a parish church in Paris by Henry Lerolle. The chair is Charles X and the carpet a 19th-century Oushak from Doris Leslie Blau.

cavalry to instruct young cavaliers as to which plants it was safe to have their horses eat," Marino explains, adding with a laugh, "People think they're just lovely flower prints, and I say, oh no, on the back it says things like, 'If your horse eats this, it'll get sick and die.' "

At the end of the hall to the master bedroom is a large Chabannes La Palice pastel of 1903, *Portrait of a Young Man:* a French aristocrat in Edwardian attire—at once world-weary and worldly-wise—is sitting at the top of some stairs leading to a library. "We put it there to give the passage greater depth and perspective," Marino explains. "You feel you can just walk right up the stairs in the picture, that somebody's actually sitting there."

The curtains in the bedroom are very thick green wool, almost like a carpet—"made by the same factory in France that made all the jackets for Napoleon's army," Marino points out. On wooden rings, they can be flipped over in summer—transformed into a green-and-white cotton stripe from a lining fabric. Two superb Persian pots from the Safavid dynasty serve as lamps on either side of the bed, their Benjamin Caldwell bronze mountings encrusted with gold filigree and semiprecious blue and red stones catching, holding, refracting the light.

All this brilliance—every moment of work, every inch of detail, every scintilla of atmosphere—was brought to full effect one evening when Marino and Whittle collected a small group of friends to sup in celebration of the apartment's completion. Golden beluga caviar, roast quail, and charlotte russe were served on imperial Russian porcelain, each plate glittering with its own royal palace in St. Petersburg. Afterward, the guests gathered round the 1870 massive rosewood piano in the living room as the Metropolitan Opera baritone Dale Duesing sang Charles Griffes's "Evening Song" and Edvard Grieg's "Ein Traum"—songs in fashion at the time the Dakota was built. For a moment the clock had stopped. Suspended in the dazzling anachronism Marino had created, where not a thing was out of resonance, one left the apartment half expecting to find a carriage and driver waiting downstairs.

McMillen
for Carolyn Farb

A reproduction Russian lantern dangles with the delicacy of a necklace above the oval entrance hall. A rare Korean chest inlaid with mother-of-pearl stands at the top of the stairs. Overleaf: The music room's variety of textures and colors merge melodiously on the patterned turf of a Sultanabad rug.

*R*hyme and reason. Carolyn Farb believes life must have both. And when she identifies the entrance hall of her Houston house as its "soul" she pinpoints the spot where a mingling of the poetic and the rational has occurred. Black and white squares hopscotch their way across the floor creating visual rhymes as they go while the precise lines and sweeping flow of a banister reach out to encircle and control them in a smooth embrace. This room, the core of a Georgian-style house built in 1940 on Houston's renowned River Oaks Boulevard, was the starting point for a massive renovation under the direction of the New York design firm McMillen, Inc. McMillen razed two-thirds of the original house and then added on to make it half again as large as it was. When they had finished giving the house the fine architectural details—classical pilasters, moldings, and mantels—that are their trademark, they filled the interior with eighteenth-century antiques from England and the Orient, handmade rugs from Poland and Portugal, and an extraordinary collection of porcelain from China. The result was not just a balance between the forces of rhyme and reason, but a harmonious blurring of the distinctions between them.

Carolyn Farb and McMillen designer Ethel Smith "clicked right away," says Farb. "One time when we were out shopping together in New York, I saw the crystal

Two views of the living room. Left: *An 18th-century mantel sports two colors of marble, pagoda valances crown silk damask curtains, and upholstered chairs mirror each other across an 18th-century English bench.* Below left: *A lacquered coffee table from China and English chairs are backed by a grand Coromandel screen, a piece from an earlier Farb house. Walls are glazed in the color of soft parchment.* Opposite: *A rare Perry chandelier sheds light on the antique silver and Georgian table. Paintings are by Georges d'Espagnat (right) and Gustave Loiseau. Bessarabian rug was copied in Poland after an 18th-century original.*

chandelier that now hangs in the dining room. I felt it look out at me and say, 'I want to come to Texas with you.' I turned around and noticed that Mrs. Smith had seen it too. She just smiled at me and said, 'Indeed, we have found a gem.' " The chandelier, Ethel Smith knew, was a rare design from the Adam period.

Such shopping expeditions were to Carolyn Farb "wonderful flights of fancy." But what she most appreciated about the McMillen designers was their sensitivity to the "mentality" of the house, its easy flow from one room to another. For the music room, which is used for entertaining, they found a magnificent Sultanabad rug that echoes the Bermudan blue of the adjacent library as well as the soft Venetian pinks of the music room.

"I love this house with a great passion," says Carolyn Farb (who has named the house Carolina) and the famous domestic sensitivity of Colette comes to mind when you see the attention she pays to the details of living well. She plants softly colored flowers outside windows to harmonize with the colors of the interior, she leaves for her houseguests bathrobes that complement the colors of their rooms, she spends hours planning the crystal, linens, and china for dinner parties so that they will never repeat themselves. She even concocts special fragrances—Eucalyptus de Versailles, Rose Exotique—to spray on the lamps in her favorite rooms. Just as McMillen has catered perfectly to her desires, so Carolyn Farb attends to living in her house, with intelligence, comfort, and style.

Left: *A painting of roses by Paul Maze and an embroidered rug from Portugal welcome houseguests to "The Rose Room."* Below left: *Bedposts and walls in the master bedroom are pasted in pale yellow satin sprinkled with polka dots. Embroidered rug is another from Portugal; chairs are Louis XV.* Opposite: *The library, lacquered in Bermudan blue, is Carolyn Farb's favorite room.*

Renzo Mongiardino for Elsa Peretti

*P*robably everyone who meets Elsa Peretti hopes to get to know her better. She is one of those ignited people whose light others want to share, and she gives the impression that she would be happy to oblige. It is no wonder that she must regularly isolate herself to design her jewelry and objects and live her life. That life, though it involves a lot of traveling, is led in a more peaceful fashion than it once was; New York sees her less and less, losing status to a tiny village in Spain, a hilltop in Italy, and her native city of Rome, a place she thought she didn't love anymore.

Elsa Peretti's apartment in the building she grew up in was where her father made his last home and office. Some years after his death, Elsa, with the apartment in her possession, decided it would be convenient to put a foot down in Rome again; she hadn't really spent time there in twenty years.

There was no time to fix up the apartment herself. Nor did she feel confident enough to do so, being attuned to the "washed" look of the countryside. She thought she would ask Renzo Mongiardino, Milan's acknowledged master of ambience, to help her: in her sister and brother-in-law's palace he had beguiled light and space. He had also seemed to be "a very nice guy."

Preceding pages:
*Over the 18th-century
fireplace in Elsa Peretti's
Rome apartment hangs a
lion cub by English
painter James Northcote
(1746–1831). Joaquim
Ros bronze on round
table is of Spanish dancer
Antonio Gades, a friend.*
Above: *An elephant
saddle from India
supports finch cages. In
the distance, the pine
trees of Villa Borghese.*
Right: *Olive branches fill
a 17th-century Verona
marble well in the living
room. Sofa by
Mongiardino and
armchairs are covered in
French cotton.*

Above: A typical Peretti still life. Chinese Buddha, coral rose, rock crystal Peretti perfume bottle in front of a chunk of that mineral, petrified mushrooms, ivory bird-feeding sticks. Opposite: A white marble torso of Elsa Peretti by Xavier Corberó is draped with her gold mesh. Precious root vase, probably Ming, holds a branch of juniper. On wall, a copy of a Roman bas-relief.

The master of ambience and Elsa Peretti were a little shy together at first; though he was "not at all imposing," he didn't say much, and as he looked around he scratched his beard in a way that made her think he didn't want to take on her small apartment. ("This is typical Mongiardino," Peretti was to learn. "Each time he scratches his beard there is something wrong.") But Mongiardino said yes, and from her brief list of favored materials and colors—terra cotta, marble, slate, black—he conjured a proposal that made her wonder how he had crept under her skin.

The apartment overlooks Villa Borghese, Rome's largest public park, and the terrace that wraps around three sides affords views of St. Peter's, the surrounding hills, the old and new glories that lie in between. Mongiardino had a celebration of all this in mind as he executed his plans; but of course his liberal interpretations and reinterpretations of classical columns, friezes, and bas-reliefs are more than that. His "patchwork of antiquity," taking in Rome's rich light, history, and art, is also his sensitive response to the apartment's owner, showing profound understanding of the sensibility that revolutionized jewelry design ten years ago. "Mongiardino likes the perfect frame," Elsa Peretti says. "If he doesn't have it he cannot work. I'm like that too, if I don't have the perfect setting for a stone. . . . These things take time, and I didn't push. I began to live very well in this apartment before everything was set up. He got the right frame, and I had a bed to sleep on." (The five years of painstaking craftsmanship that went into this apartment were overseen by Mongiardino's right-hand man in Rome, Bruno Carlino, also a nice and "very Roman kind of guy.")

Is it possible that a physical environment can reveal someone to herself? Reintroduced to the flavors of a city she had left behind, Elsa Peretti feels she has been given the luxury of home. "This apartment is for life, for the future—for my life and for the next people who have it, because, you see, I have the feeling it is a classic."

Above: *In dining room,
Empire chairs, two
Mongiardino tables of
various marbles, petrified
wood. Viennese painted-
bronze dog on steps. On
tables, scroll by
Tsuruugawa T'anyu, Edo
period; Peretti plate, and
vase. Opposite: Coral
necklaces spill from an
Etruscan cup. Falcon is
one panel of a
Japanese screen.*

Above: *Falcon-screen panels flank an Imari plate by George O'Brien for Tiffany & Co. Small objects in and on shelf include cricket cages, evening bags and lacquer bean by Peretti, jade cigarette holder.* Right: *Gazebo by Mongiardino echoes cupola of St. Peter's. Terra-cotta acorns, vases by Tobie Loup de Viane, who transformed terrace planting. Gate from an old convent.* Far right: *Circa-1670 Roman cabinet in bedroom, whose mate is in living room, was influenced by Borromini. On it, a T'ang lady-in-waiting.*

Parish-Hadley for Enid Annenberg Haupt

For decades, Enid Annenberg Haupt has lived the sort of life others want to have. Equally celebrated as a gardener and an art collector, she has nevertheless managed to maintain a rich and private inner life. Shy of the camera, she is photographed only on the sly at the best benefits. The houses and apartments she has arranged for herself, on the other hand, have been published with regularity, forming enviable—and imitated—documents in the history of recent taste. "Sometimes florists say to me, 'For God's sakes, you caused us such trouble,'" Mrs. Haupt relates. "People come to them with tear sheets and say, 'I want my rooms to look just like Mrs. Haupt's.' They say, 'Well that's very easily done—if you just have three sets of plants and each week have someone to take them out to a greenhouse.'"

She is standing in her light- and flower-filled penthouse on Manhattan's East Side. Although space is often said to be New York's greatest luxury, surely the quality of light here, coming from all points of the compass, is an even greater one. More luxurious still, because of their ephemeral nature, are the flowers, or rather, the flowering plants that Mrs. Haupt was among the first in America to bring indoors. Her favorite orchids are here in profusion all

Curtains of unlined taffeta from Clarence House billow in the breeze in Enid Haupt's penthouse apartment in New York. The Tiepolo frescoes on canvas are part of a suite of fifteen.

year round. According to the season, they are complemented by cyclamen, tulips, roses, or a sort of topiary chrysanthemum that gives the lie to anyone who thinks of that flower as common. "There's nothing ordinary about *my* chrysanthemums," Mrs. Haupt says.

The most surprising change from her former décors is the absence of the remarkable collection of Impressionist and Postimpressionist paintings that once provoked Douglas Cooper, the great collector and connoisseur of Cubism, to remark to Mrs. Haupt, "Your paintings and mine should go off and make babies together." Instead, rather more incestuously, they joined the collection of her brother, Walter Annenberg, in Palm Springs, to form the basis of a future museum. The "deaccessioning," as Mrs. Haupt calls it, was not total; she retained a Vuillard screen in the library, and an extraordinary series of Tiepolo frescoes on canvas in grisaille and gold were moved from the entrance hall to the living room. The Metropolitan Museum displays eleven similar Tiepolos; Mrs. Haupt has fifteen.

"There was a prominent, prominent executive of the Metropolitan here one night," she remarks, "and he said, 'People would be shocked to hear this but I like it better without the modern paintings.' And I said, 'But so do I!' " Still, nothing looks more "modern" than a room like Mrs. Haupt's drawing room, composed almost entirely of eighteenth-century elements. Gone are the plain white walls that were once a background for the art; in their place are richly and unashamedly "decorated" surfaces, which Mrs. Haupt admits are a first for her. "I'd never used a decorator before, you see," she says. "I'd never even had curtains. I just had plants, plants, plants—and the paintings. But I'd always say to Sister socially, 'If I ever do a new scene, will you help me?' And when it came time to do it, she did."

She refers, of course, to Mrs. Henry Parish II, the redoubtable "Sister," as she is known to the *gratin* of Manhattan. In Mrs. Haupt, she encountered an equally formidable presence. On her first visit, Mrs. Haupt recalls, Mrs. Parish brought a swatch of flowered chintz to see if it was the sort of thing she wanted. It delighted her, but what delighted her even more was that it turned out to be the chintz that Mrs. Parish has used for herself for twenty years. In other ways, the two women's tastes proved remarkably compatible. They both like Bessarabian and Savonnerie rugs, for instance. Both favor the same mix of French, English, and Italian furniture, much of it painted and most of it eighteenth century in origin, although both have a special fondness for the early-nineteenth-century pieces that resulted "when Nappy came back from Egypt," as Mrs. Haupt

Opposite: *A Diego Giacometti lamp stands next to a Louis XVI chair in the entrance hall.* Above: *Another view of the entrance hall, its wall marbleized by Robert Jackson.* Overleaf: *In the living room, the "roundabout" covered in Scalamandré silk anchors two groupings of Louis XV and Louis XVI furniture. The chandelier is Russian, the mirrors English.*

Above: *Tiepolo frescoes from a Venetian palace were transferred to canvas. The living room sofa is covered in Mrs. Haupt's—and Mrs. Parish's—favorite flowered chintz from Lee Jofa.* Opposite: *In the sitting/dining room, one of a pair of Louis XVI settees is surrounded by flowers.*

puts it. They diverged, in fact, only on one point. Mrs. Parish urged her client to restore the fireplaces to the rooms; Mrs. Haupt explained that she had had them removed herself because smoke is bad for plants. Such are her priorities.

Admiring the look of flowerpots on bare floors, she also asked that the parquet de Versailles in the living room be left exposed. Anchoring this room is one of the few new pieces of furniture in the apartment, that modish example of the upholsterer's art for which no one seems to agree on a name, calling it variously a "borne," a "confidante," or a "roundabout," as Albert Hadley, Mrs. Parish's partner, would have it. This example was copied from one Nancy Lancaster had at Haseley Court.

"I call it my little 'conversational,' " Mrs. Haupt says, now perched upon it in her drawing room. "I was at Haseley Court maybe twenty years ago. Nancy was away but I'd gone to see the topiary chess set because I had a topiary garden at the time. Anyway, the caretaker said, 'Would you care to see the house?' and I said, 'I'd adore to,' always having been mad about houses, and then. . . 'Oh!' I said, 'This is divine!' For years I just kept it as a lovely memory. But that house had a place in my mind. And when I deaccessioned my art collection it was the opportunity to have the English country house look on the elegant basis I'd always wanted."

She remembers that when she first started growing orchids she had to send to England for the bulbs. Her decision, long ago, to adopt the English use of terra-cotta pots indoors was an attempt, she says, "to bring an earthy feeling to a rich feeling." Her ideas about gardening, in fact, bear the same English influence as Parish-Hadley's ideas about decoration, and complement them, having the same hallmarks: expensive simplicity, a deliberate downplaying of grandeur, and a contrived apparent lack of contrivance. Although Mrs. Haupt's apartment was basically a "cosmetic" job, nothing Parish-Hadley applies its talents to could really be so characterized. The walls were variously "dragged, stippled, and *glazed*," in Mrs. Parish's words, not to mention marbleized by the incomparable Robert Jackson. The flowing unlined silk taffeta curtains were mocked up in muslin and then realized with an attention to detail that Mrs. Parish likens to old-fashioned Parisian dress-making, while Mrs. Haupt, in Albert Hadley's words, oversaw "every gimp, tassel, and ribbon," almost all of which were custom-made. "It was just as if she were back at the magazine," Mrs. Parish says, referring to her client's tenure as the editor of *Seventeen*. "A perfectionist," she adds, now almost purring, acknowledging a kindred soul.

"I *was* very meticulous about what was printed under my name as an editor," Mrs. Haupt comments. "And I had an electrified magnifying glass and saw things that the art department never saw. You see, I have that kind of pride." She is now sitting in the library. Once a dining room, it has become her favorite room to be alone in. "I truly *live* here," she says. "The kind of social life that takes people out every night has never interested me. I'd rather read. I'm having a wonderful time now, for instance, learning about rain forests." There follows an extended digression on the subject bristling with learned statistics. "Where else would you learn about this if you weren't reading about rain forests all the time?" she asks.

Invariably, her thoughts return to nature, and in particular to her flowers, "my friends, my companions, and my children." Still, for someone who has never had curtains before, she shows a genuine appreciation of artifice. "It's such a marvelous turn of events for me to have this whole new atmosphere," she says. "I must say when the sun comes through the curtains. . . I'm pulling their skirts out all the time. And people say, 'Oh, aren't you afraid of what the sun will do?' I say, 'As long as there's still Paris and I still have a few pennies to scrape together. . . I'm going to have my unlined silk taffeta!' "

In the library Mrs. Haupt
asked for a "café au lait"
feeling. "A certain range
of color," she says, is
constant in her taste.
That range also includes
the furniture in this
room, all "a kind of pale
walnut, the beechwood of
the French." Rug is
Bessarabian, screen is
by Vuillard.

Above: *The sitting/dining room is used for light meals; Dresden china sets the table. Drawings are old master Italian. Opposite: The bedroom, reflected in an 18th-century trumeau mirror, is done in Lee Jofa chintz. Headboard and hangings in pale blue silk were appliquéd with French ribbons by Brunschwig especially for Mrs. Haupt. In foreground are 18th-century Venetian silk-embroidered religious subjects in painted frames.*

Piero Pinto
for Laura Biagiotti

*F*rom the beginning, there could have been nothing but romance between the castle of Marco Simone and fashion designer Laura Biagiotti. At their first encounter, in 1977, "a kind of madness" seized Biagiotti. She hesitated briefly but knew deep down that she and this house belonged together. Then, with the decision made, came the "betrothal," four years filled with hard work and the joy of anticipating for herself, her family, and her entire business staff an extraordinary establishment. Like any worthwhile betrothal, this one was a happy adventure, luckily free of trauma, but rich in turning points and dramatic events.

The restoration is the achievement of Piero Pinto, an expert and sensitive architect/interior designer and a man who is utterly intolerant of artistic deceit. "At the beginning," says Piero Pinto, "we found ourselves confronted with a big ruin—fascinating, but still a ruin. The first job, itself very demanding, was to know where to start, which things to value, which to sacrifice." Apart from the difficulty of unraveling the tangled superimpositions of various periods, there were early problems involving traffic. Between the ground floor and the one above (the route to the

Preceding pages:
*Marco Simone castle,
whose substructure
contains columns and
inscriptions of Imperial
Rome. The tower is 14th
century, the wings 15th
century, the corner
fortifications 16th. The
Baroque portal leads from
the main courtyard into
an internal one. Behind
arched windows: a
reopened loggia. Right:
Piero Pinto designed the
drawing room floor in
three zones, marked by
borders of travertine
around areas of terra
cotta. Frescoes from the
15th century dominate
the room. Large
cupboards from the
former sacristy now
store books.*

tower), no indoor connection existed, only an outside stair. In a more advanced stage of work, Pinto came to understand, half by induction, half by intuition, that such a passage had to have existed and probably had been buried. "Without it the house would not have been fit to live in, in the past or now." He gave orders to excavate and his theory was confirmed. It was then that he knew he would achieve his aim of giving the severe old ruin the comforts of home—to domesticate it, in a word, while conserving its artistic and historic worth.

In one case of superimposition, fifteenth-century frescoes were covered by nineteenth-century neo-Gothic paintings. In certain places the later work was crumbling, and Biagiotti herself, while scraping a small piece on a Sunday afternoon, discovered the first little painted column. In demolishing partitions of a later epoch, which subdivided the upper *salone* into three rooms, another painted column and part of a small, delicious landscape emerged. From these discoveries came the decision to scrape away all the neo-Gothic pictures, the banal and even the pleasant. Most of the painted rooms were decreed by Pinto to remain rigorously empty—rooms of passage inhabited only by the rediscovered frescoes and whoever stopped to admire them. In one room four feminine medallion portraits, including one of Cleopatra, probably date back to ancient Rome and might have been removed from some great villa of the region. Other frescoes from the fifteenth century

reappeared when the loggia was reopened. These paintings depict the four cardinal virtues and four divinities, in addition to naturalistic motifs, and reveal the most felicitous hand. Frescoes on sacred subjects were found in the former chapel and moved to the huge white drawing room: Saint Rocco and Saint Antonio Abate, both much invoked in the fourteenth and fifteenth centuries as protectors against the plague.

In the course of the long effort, Pinto's work was much facilitated by the valuable collaboration of the local workmen and the foreman, Vincenzo Jacopini; he was also in love with the old pile of stones and presented a new discovery as a gift to Pinto and Biagiotti every time they inspected the work. A group of restorers spent almost an entire year in the castle, weathering a difficult winter, to patiently attend the healthy rebirth of the antique frescoes. Architect Maurizio Cagnoni also collaborated, especially in the construction of the factory at the foot of the castle. As one can imagine, it was difficult not to break into the castle walls to install the electricity, but Piero Castiglioni, in charge of the lighting, succeeded in placing cables in the attic.

Piero Pinto and Laura Biagiotti share the opinion that any sign of luxury is out of place in a country castle; Pinto chose materials long used in the region: recycled brick and roof tiles, travertine, terra cotta, and on the walls, the so-called *stucco Romano,* or *pozzolana* (marble powder, gesso, cement, and clay bound with a method dis-

Left: *Presiding over the second-floor drawing room, an 18th-century marble statue in the Roman style represents Summer. In the 1500s Federico Cesi I did an enormous remodeling here and had his name inscribed on numerous door lintels. Pinto regrouped them all in this room.* Below left: *White tiles of various shapes make a rug-patterned floor for the white drawing room on the lower level. The contemporary furnishings display the spirit of superimposition that marks the castle's long history. Beyond the American primitive bird is one of the saintly fresoes found in the former chapel.*

covered at the time of Pompeii). White ceramic tiles of a particular transparency form a decorative pavement that has become one of the trademarks of Pinto's work. At Marco Simone, this tile has a special grace, for it softens the sternness of the castle. Laura Biagiotti's followers know that white is her preferred noncolor.

The preservation of the work of diverse periods helped guard against "doing" the castle "in style." The furniture was chosen eclectically, so that styles would be combined as naturally as in an old family house where each generation leaves it mark. Thus, important French sofas of the nineteenth century are fronted by furniture made today; a seventeenth-century altar stands near some "Paolo Uccello" chairs put into production at Simon International in 1981, both under a delicious eighteenth-century Venetian chandelier. Everything comes together as intended, with an effect of casualness, of elegant offhandedness, and above all, of freedom from rules.

Now the castle of Marco Simone is a house where it is pleasant to live and to be employed—the happy ending to this story of love and work. All the collaborators can feel the satisfaction of having contributed to the restoration and salvation of a tangible testimony to art and history, and by making Marco Simone alive again, Laura Biagiotti can sink her roots in a remote past whose solid foundations should have an equally durable future. To someone who works in the ephemeral world of fashion, all this has special meaning.

Above: *The tower
contains guest rooms such
as one whose dressing
area includes a Second
Empire chest.* Opposite:
*In Laura Biagiotti's
bedroom the large space
and its stony surfaces had
to be softened and made
more welcoming. Piero
Pinto veiled some of the
walls, the windows, and
the bed with white silk,
actually a dress fabric.
The bed, an 1830
Viennese piece, creates a
room within the room.*

Andrée Putman
for Harry Hunt

Harry Hunt's third-floor flat in a 1936 building on Telegraph Hill in San Francisco is reached via a suave spiral staircase leading to a spacious entry hall at the center of the apartment. Overleaf, left: The architect's clear volumes are mirrored and discreetly underscored by Eileen Gray's Mediterranée rug, reproduced by Andrée Putman's Ecart International. Overleaf, right: The living room viewed from the terrace.

*A*ndrée Putman's astounding success since the founding of her design firm, Ecart International, derives from her intuition that a significant public felt disenfranchised from most of what her co-professionals were offering at the time. Unwilling to accept either the historicist fantasies of the traditionalists or the minimalists' denial of the senses, that public has found in Andrée Putman a voice for its unfulfilled desires: rooms informed by modern history and yet unmistakably contemporary, with luxury tempered by discretion and comfort.

Among the Putman constituency is Harry Hunt, a San Franciscan with particular interests in motorcycles (which he has built and raced professionally) and the vanguard design of this century. About the same time that Andrée Putman launched Ecart, Harry Hunt bought a three-story villa on Telegraph Hill, built in 1936 to the designs of the architect Gardner Dailey for his personal use. The new owner's vision for the refurbishing of the upper of the building's two apartments for himself was a simple but distinguished scheme that would both defer to and enhance the architectural essence of the structure, a fine example of the modernist style gracefully adapted to the characteristic human scale and varied texture of the San Francisco cityscape.

Andrée Putman was intrigued by both this client and his house. She has created domestic interiors for a wide variety of settings, ranging from a Paris loft to a Park Avenue apartment, but none of them has offered her a context so close in form and spirit to her own favorite period, the 1920s and '30s. Especially to her taste was the building's basic restraint, for although she is fond of Art Deco and Art Moderne, she can easily dispense with the kitschy excesses of those ornamented styles. Her strategy drew upon a number of her by-now-familiar principles—uncluttered surfaces, neutral colors, and classic furniture of her own manufacture arranged in striking juxtapositions—but it nevertheless seems fresh and fitting. Furthermore, it manages to satisfy several requirements at once: appropriateness for the place, respect for the architecture, and pleasure for the inhabitant.

The apartment is entered through a small street-level vestibule in which stands an Ecart reproduction of the Scots-Irish early-modern designer Eileen Gray's ingenious pivot-drawer bureau of chrome and black lacquer. A spiral staircase with a sleek white-metal banister (beautifully restored by Harry Hunt) leads up to his flat on the top floor. The rooms are not as big as some contempo-

Above: *Overlooking the bay, the living room has Eileen Gray's Transat chairs and Black Board rug. Limed-oak table copies a Jean Michel Frank design.* Opposite: *Mariano Fortuny lamp dominates dining room corner.* Overleaf: *In the master bath, Gray's Satellite mirror beneath Hoffmannesque tile frieze.*

rary California interiors, serving as a reminder of the intimate scale typical of early-modern architecture before it took an increasingly institutional turn in the years after World War II. But even without immense dimensions, the living room seems expansive thanks to large windows that open onto spectacular, 180-degree views of San Francisco Bay, its bridges, and its islands, and to a terrace on its eastern end that can be used most of the year.

Wherever possible, elements that were original to the house were retained, such as the chaste and chic black marble fireplace surround in the living room, the white-metal indirect lighting fixture suspended from the ceiling of the stair tower, and the black-stained oak parquet flooring. With basics so similar to those she would have proposed had they not been there, Andrée Putman could focus on refining the areas that needed the most attention after over forty years of continuous use by the original occupants.

Among them were the bathrooms, and these she has bestowed with the beautifully detailed functionalism that qualifies her as one of the most skilled practition-

ers of an interior design specialty that so easily veers off into nouveau glitz. The master bath is a case in point: tiled in pure white, it is circumscribed by a double frieze of blue and black tiles, four small blue ones below each large black one. The effect brings to mind the checked-border motif much used by the designers of the Wiener Werkstätte—another major source of Andrée Putman's inspiration. That derivation is underscored here by her choice of the pierced-metal grid soap holder and wastebasket designed by Josef Hoffmann, founder of that Viennese group.

Her black-granite-topped washstand, on the other hand, with its forthrightly off-the-shelf metal fittings reminiscent of the twenties, could just as well have been put together by Le Corbusier for one of his famous cubist villas of that decade outside Paris. Eileen Gray's spectacular Satellite mirror—a small universe of intersecting circles bringing to mind a reflective Delaunay—completes the composition as the perfect counterpoint to this high-tech but low-profile luxe.

What has been accomplished in this project proves once again the wisdom of Andrée Putman's convic-tion that there is no such thing as a truly convincing period room, whether it be Marie Antoinette or Moderne. She believes that the world inevitably understands the past in terms of the present, and that attempts at overliteral re-creations of historic styles are doomed to failure. With modernism being viewed in some quarters as a completed phase in architecture—a premise that Andrée Putman's work at least partially belies—the question of how to "cor-rectly" furnish rooms built in that mode is upon us.

During the heyday of the International Style in the fifties and sixties, a very limited, predictable range of "acceptable" interior design choices hastened the rejection of modernism. Andrée Putman's admirable endeavors to widen our sense of the modernist experience—exempli-fied in this first-rate scheme—indicate that one need not indulge in either revivalism or repudiation if one wants to carry on in the innovative tradition of our waning century. "It is all that I wanted, and more," says Harry Hunt of his apartment, and his and his designer's ability to read be-tween the very clean lines of his rooms is the secret of their mutual success.

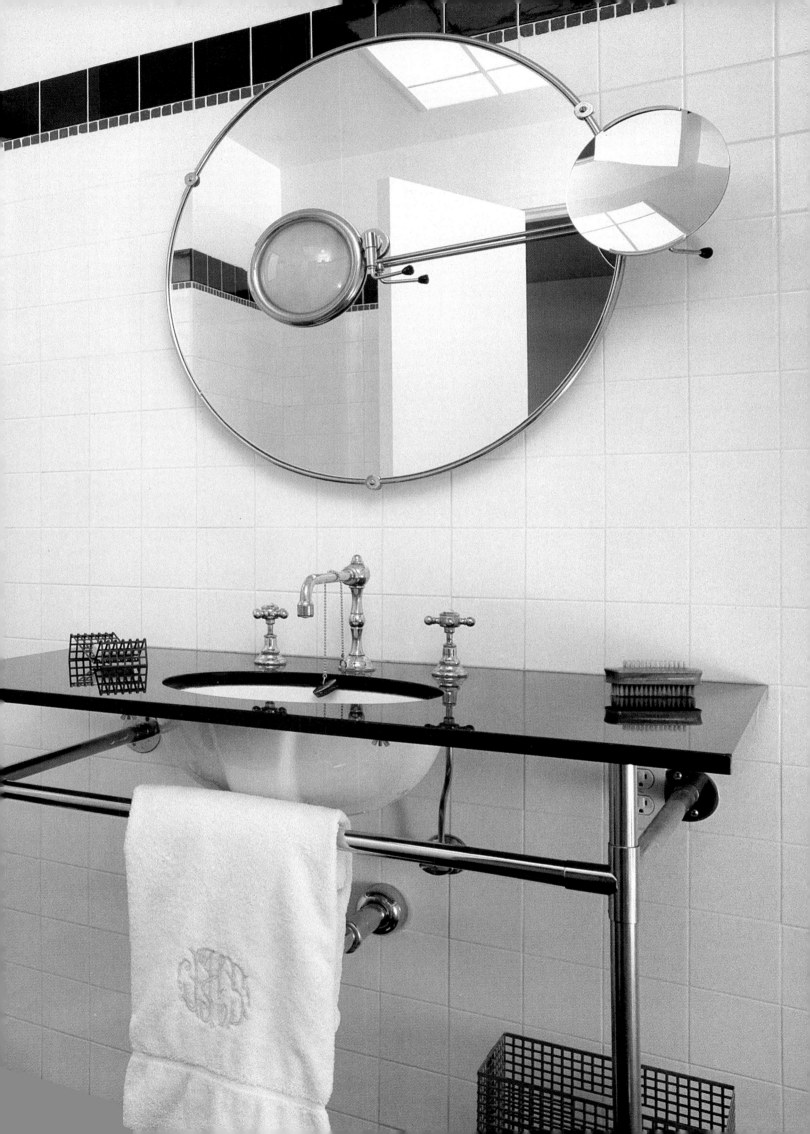

Michael Taylor for Diana and Gorham Knowles

*F*or two thousand summers the Washo Indians camped around the Nevada and California shores of Lake Tahoe, leaving only the occasional arrowhead to suggest their seasonal presence. In the 150 years since the white man came upon this phantasmagoria of blue/green/gray/black water set into the granite ranges of the Sierra Nevada, Tahoe's rare beauty has almost been its undoing.

Yet from Gorham and Diana Dollar Knowles's property at Homewood, midway on the 22-mile length of the lake on the California side, the sprawl of Tahoe development doesn't seem to apply. Studded with firs and pines, sloping steeply down to a sheltered cove, the Knowleses' place at "the lake" (which can only mean Tahoe to those from "the city," which can only mean San Francisco) is a pristine miracle of survival.

For the Knowles family it is a matter of total recall. Both Mr. and Mrs. Knowles are native San Franciscans who summered at the lake with their familes as long as they can remember. Their early days at Tahoe were idyllic; it was a time when lake steamers with mail and visitors made ports of call at campgrounds and family docks, and

Silhouetted against Lake Tahoe, 18th-century Japanese wood deer graze near Michael Taylor's round ash dining table for twelve.

On walls of cedar siding in the living room hang a twig construction by Charles Arnoldi and a pair of 19th-century Austrian metal-and-horn deer heads. Raw-rock coffee table stands before sofa upholstered in handwoven chenille. Michael Taylor designed all the upholstered pieces and benches for the room.

the new two-lane paved roads linking the various lake colonies were assumed to be more than adequate forever.

A 1930 wood-hull Gar Wood speedboat named *Tamarack,* now docked at the end of the Knowleses' pier, is redolent of those halcyon years. "Diana's father gave *Tamarack* to her when she was a very young girl," says Gorham Knowles, "and it's been in the water here every summer since." The prized 28-foot classic is still piloted as it always was, to visit friends of a lifetime around the lake. It has also effected a further continuity in lending its name to the new Knowles spread, dubbed Tamarack Cove.

A few years before the Knowleses found their present place, previous owners had gutted the original house and rebuilt it in redwood, retaining the robust native-stone fireplaces and introducing full-height panels of glass angled to vistas of the ever-moving lake and to the tapestries of trees that screen Tamarack Cove on three sides. So seductive are the various prospects from the house, even after a lifetime of Tahoe summers, says Diana Knowles, that "we had to put shutters on the bedroom windows because we were up all night admiring the view."

For their alfresco life at the lake, with children, grandchildren, and friends, the Knowleses added a redwood deck on the living room level and, down the slope, a munificent spread of a terrace in native granite as varying in tone as Lake Tahoe itself, which overlooks their

Preceding pages: *At the end of Diana and Gorham Knowles's pier is moored a 1930 wood-hull Gar Wood speedboat, a girlhood present from Mrs. Knowles's father.* Left: *Michael Taylor designed all the furniture in the library. Tabletops are stone mill wheels. Over fireplace, a ceremonial Indian skirt from Santa Fe.* Opposite: *Native stone terrace is an alfresco base camp between house and cove. Teakwood furniture is from Thailand.*

own secluded four-hundred-foot cove. "And no one can ever take that view away," says Gorham Knowles fervently. All of this—the nostalgia, the sense of place and passing time, the subtleties of tone and texture on the land and lake—seems distilled in the interiors that Michael Taylor designed for Tamarack Cove before his death in 1986.

A California native himself, Michael Taylor was rightly known as the creator of a "California look," his own idiosyncratic vernacular that drew on a world of allusions. With their immediately perceived comfort, Michael Taylor's rooms appear as easy to read as they are to be in. But then the subtexts!

At Tamarack Cove, where colors are taken from the tones of indigenous grasses, tree bark, and sandy coves, there is also an underlying sense of continuity expressed with the strategic period piece or elemental element linking this contemporary house with time past—the nineteenth-century English gate-leg table and carved wood bear hat rack in the entry, for example, or the stone mill wheels that are used both as sculptural objects and tabletops in the library.

There's also continuity of a decorative sort in the undulating texture of the handwoven wool carpet that is reiterated in the overscale woven reeds used for the seats of Taylor's timeless pine benches and stools and also for the seats of the bleached-oak chairs pulled up to Taylor's convivial round ash dining table.

Of course, it wouldn't be a Michael Taylor interior without the sort of dramatic punch he introduced here with the enormous raw rock of a coffee table (swung in by crane) set before a sweeping sofa covered in velvety handwoven chenille.

This was not the first time that Taylor had worked with Diana Knowles, and knowing the family, the designer understood not only how the lake house would figure in their full social calendar but also all that Tahoe evoked to them. Michael Taylor once said, "Some of the most creative things I've ever done have come from the stimulation of a client like Diana Knowles." Living with the designer's enhancement of their world, Gorham and Diana Knowles will remember Michael Taylor with admiration in kind.

Part II
Designers at Home

"Style" in decoration is every bit as slippery as "taste"; nonetheless, we can safely say that a combination of tastes is what creates a certain style. As an artist employs the same quirky brushstroke to paintings of different subjects, so a decorator reveals the possibilities of his or her style by working for different clients. And in the same way that we eagerly examine the self-portraits of artists, we anticipate looking into designers' own rooms: Are they the key to what makes decorators tick, to what most influences their work, and, most pertinent here, to what helps us define our own aesthetic? The answer is yes, and the reason is deceptively simple: decorators know what they like, and they know how to get it. In Part Two of our book, we show you the results.

Confident of their likes and dislikes, decorators are always open to challenge, and their inspiration can come from what might be considered unusual sources. Stephen Sills grew up in Oklahoma imagining the contours and colors of much more exotic places, and the child's imagination still operates through the adult: in Sills's decorating "laboratory" in Dallas, "illusion and reality cross tracks so often that the eye soon learns to assume nothing and imagine anything." Jacques Grange, who romanticized about living in a certain Paris apartment for years, through patience and luck finally got it. His idea of honoring the rooms came in an instinctive response: "the cozy domesticity of a Vuillard painting." John Saladino, always interested in the breadth of architectural history, wanted a "civilized ruin"/ "space-time continuum" in a historic apartment in New York City, and with the scrupulous attention he is known to pay to detail and craftsmanship, he achieved a postmodern spectacle that has room as well to reflect his family's domestic and aesthetic proclivities.

For her clients, Suzie Frankfurt devises interiors with English and French furniture, but for herself she had imagined since childhood having "her own Russia." With study, lucky purchases, and thoughts of Tolstoy and Pushkin, she has created the perfect "stage set for her imagination." The real France, or at least his part of it, eventually crossed the Atlantic when Vincent Fourcade brought to Long Island the massive Art Nouveau furniture from his childhood home outside Paris. The decorator's confidence in the integrity of these pieces meant he could "let the furniture tell the house what to do."

Family history and feeling were also important to Arnold Copper's farmhouse in New England and Renzo Mongiardino's apartment in Milan. For Copper, who specializes in strict historical preservation, a house that went back as far as his American heritage naturally had appeal, but the likable "compromises" various owners had given the house over three hundred years invited him to add his own quirks and use certain favored things and materials where they didn't "belong." Mongiardino was after the mood rather than the reality of his parents' *palazzo,* and by mixing some of his parents' well-worn and old-fashioned things with much fakery, he contrived rooms with a comfortable, "deliberately *délabré* patina and nostalgic air"—also illustrating how "deceit is his secret weapon."

Like Mongiardino, Henri Samuel—"the decorator's decorator"—has a reputation for creating sumptuous settings for extraordinary historical treasures. These settings often reflect one period; his own rooms embrace his love of cross-cultural, cross-calendar travel—intriguing juxtapositions of works of art and furniture from many times, many places, all navigated by a decorator who never loses his way.

Navigating the future inspired Barbara Schwartz's decoration of the apartment she shares with her husband, Eugene. That they are collectors of contemporary art means their collection is often changing, and Mrs. Schwartz's versatile furnishings assure that the apartment as an entirety has an anchor in timelessness. In contrast to the Schwartzes, Mica Ertegun looks to the future as a time when she *will* redecorate in entirety—not for the first time. Knowing her tastes will change, her talents grow, she believes that in reflecting life, "a house has to be a living thing—it should never be finished." Mica Ertegun does have a period of repose between redecorations. "After all," she says—and her statement can apply broadly to all of us—"I can't demand more than what I've chosen for myself."

Benjamin Baldwin

By adding partitions, Ben Baldwin made himself a Persian-inspired walled garden that unfolds as one passes through it. He also built the exposed aggregate path, which he loves to walk at night, and the shaded seating area.

*T*he tides of decorating fashion ebb and flood—wild pattern-on-pattern followed by steely high tech, casual English country followed by ornate *style Rothschild*—but Benjamin Baldwin goes his steady, comfortable, classical-contemporary way. His way convinced architect Louis Kahn to elect Baldwin his interior designer for several projects, and Edward Larabee Barnes chose him to decorate the library and dining areas of the Dallas Museum of Art.

The Alabama-born designer of interiors, buildings, furniture, and gardens spent a postgraduate year at Cranbrook Academy with architect Eliel Saarinen in the late thirties, and it is the Cranbrook modernist influence—gentle, eclectic, humane—that is most evident in Ben Baldwin's work. In his house in Sarasota, Florida, his fireplace alone could sum up the style: a once-hokey barbecue installation now stripped clean and standing free, adorned only by a locally made iron fork and a South Pacific shield. His primitive art and other pieces are choice but few in number. "I am not a collector. I can say good-bye to something if it crowds me."

"Clutter and fashion do not interest me at all," Baldwin continues. "My design has always followed the same direction; there are certain basic things that are right, no matter when they are done, and those things are many. But they have to come from somebody's very strong personal feelings."

Above: *The waterside façade of the Sarasota house is framed by mangroves.* Right: *Back-to-back sofas were designed by Baldwin. In this arrangement, one is used by day, one by night.*

Left: *The dining corner of the big main space overlooks the moon-viewing deck. Dining table and chairs by Ben Baldwin.* Below left: *The trim kitchen has a Matisse paper frieze.* Right: *Site-built lattice at windows has small gauge; behind outdoor lunch table, gauge of lattice is far larger to vary the geometry.*

In both East Hampton, New York, and Sarasota, Baldwin has acted upon his very strong feeling that houses and gardens are inseparable, he says. "I am a gardener and I think of my houses as garden shelters."

The Florida house stands on the mangrove-rimmed edge of a Gulf inlet in a dazzling stillness broken only by the splash of jumping mullet. Baldwin bought the house for its "water, privacy, and southern exposure for gardening." He also liked the building's dilapidated condition, which meant he could "tear it apart without a qualm." As for the "garden," it was all bare earth.

Visually extending the various parts of the house into garden "rooms" was a task that was only natural to Baldwin. "Designing an interior and designing a garden are, to me, very much alike. You are dealing with plants in one, furniture in the other, but in both you work with the relation of different spaces, as well as solids and voids. It's an architectural problem, concerning shapes, volumes, masses, textures, and colors."

After two remodelings and ceaseless garden work, the now luxurious property is in a state of relative completion—as much as nature and a designer's alert eye will allow.

Arnold Copper

*T*en generations ago a William Copper from Oxfordshire settled in Virginia, and there have been Coppers on farms there or in Maryland ever since. Arnold Copper, the descendant in question, grew up on a Virginia farm, and he still regards himself as a man of the country although he is now based in an apartment and office on the Upper East Side of Manhattan, practicing as an architectural designer who specializes in historic restoration. For him real time is measured in year-round weekends and vacations on a 160-acre farm in coastal New England, which he shares with a large herd of wild deer, eight Arabian and Appaloosa horses that graze on the pastures he rents out, and his own numerous dogs and cats. Arnold Copper's farmhouse is also a family center, where his mother, siblings, and daughter gather for all the holidays, Christmas being the favorite.

The history of the house goes back almost as far as the colonial Coppers. There was only a keeping room and a small chamber in the earliest days—about 1700, plus or minus a decade—and these remain. Once the big room was the center of daily life, with its huge fireplace for warmth and for cooking on the hearth and in the beehive oven. It is still the room where host and guests spend the most time.

In 1750 a prosperous dairy farmer incorpo-

rated the original two rooms into a symmetrical five-bay, two-story Georgian house. Ninety years later, more rooms were added, as well as a side porch with two-story columns. Finally, in the late 1940s, an architect-owner built on a twenty-by-forty-foot ballroom. Copper has furnished this as a living room, but once, to honor the past, he gave a ball there, ending with a big Southern-style midnight breakfast.

The casual imperfection of this house, which has known so many years of use, additions, repairs, mistakes, corrections, and compromises revealed in funny jogs and alcoves and mismatched floors, is a source of pleasure to the designer. He explains, "In preservation work, I am required to follow strict conventions of historical style, but a house like this allows me to decorate as I please." Thus he felt free to use curtain types invented 150 years after a room's date of construction, to place a bed made for a fourteen-foot-high room under and almost touching an eight-foot ceiling, to paint his staircase one strong color—treads and risers, balusters and railing, and even the upstairs landing.

Speaking of his decorating style, Arnold Copper says his rooms are sometimes described as "looking unfinished," which he considers a compliment. He regards interiors as a process, changing as life within them changes. "If you come back here some day, you may see that I have rebuilt the plaster ceiling missing in the dining room, and some of the furniture will surely have been moved around and some materials replaced." Nevertheless, you would undoubtedly see the stylistic unity that is such a strong feature of Arnold Copper's house, a unity resulting from his almost exclusive use of American antiques (inherited and collected), a unity owing most of all to an inbred knowledge of what a nice old farmhouse ought to look and feel like.

Preceding pages: *The
circa-1700 keeping room
is part of the original
core of a much-enlarged
farmhouse.* Opposite:
*The bluish green staircase
in the 1750 part of the
house is of a vigorous
color known to be true to
the colonial period.*
Above: *During the 1940s
a large Federal-style
ballroom was added to
the house. It now
functions as a
comfortable living room.*

Preceding pages: *In the
dining room, family
fiddle-thread silver,
Coalport china. Table is a
Boston piece. Still life
paintings are American.*
Opposite above: *View
from a horse pasture to
the 1760 façade.*
Opposite below: *Master
bedroom contains a
Cuban bed handed down
through Arnold Copper's
New Orleans maternal
branch. Empire chest of
drawers from
Massachusetts.* Above: *In
a guest room, fringed
canopy is real fishnet.
China Trade recamier has
its old caning.*

A spectrum of cool whites in the Erteguns' sparely elegant second-floor living room. The focus here: Magritte's L'Empire des lumières, 1954. At left, an Empire chair.

Mica Ertegun

Would you consider this a contemporary room?'' asks the elegant Rumanian-born decorator Mica Ertegun. *Mica* means small in Rumanian and small she appears standing in the immensity of her living room, which takes up the entire second floor of the Erteguns' Upper East Side Manhattan town house. "It's very contemporary. And yet there isn't one modern thing in it," she points out triumphantly. "Most people who walk in here say, 'This is so modern.' But then, finally, it's not. Even the Kelly is becoming an old master," she laughs, with a nod toward Ellsworth Kelly's monumental *York,* which hangs over the William IV table.

Mica has allotted the generous space (the living room was originally three rooms) to create, along with the islands of privacy she was striving for, no less than five seating areas: gathering places for the large groups the Erteguns regularly entertain. A social historian once described these parties as having about them a "sense of ambitious juxtapositions." Witness the array of signed photographs on the shelves: Fred Astaire, Henry Kissinger, Mick Jagger and Jerry Hall, President and Mrs. Reagan, Ray Charles.

"My old living room had a problem," Mica says. "It's long and narrow and the seating in the middle didn't work. But when I found this pair of huge back-to-back sofas, that was the beginning of the new living room—I knew that they would be the main seating area. They're Biedermeier, but I don't care what they are. They just suited me, I like them."

Mica is a woman who knows what she likes. What George W. S. Trow, Jr., wrote of her in 1978 in his two-part *New Yorker* profile of her husband, Ahmet, chairman of Atlantic Records and "the Greatest Rock-and-Roll Mogul in the World," easily still applies: "She is contained within a strong outline of handsome appearance which is able to resist dissipation or diffusion of any kind. To Ahmet's dense strength she adds surface."

"I cannot stand the chintz look," she declares. "I knew that that was never going to be me. And I don't think it's good to go back into Victoriana or Napoleon III, although I admire and love old things." Mica is driven by the will to perfection. "My husband accuses me of changing the house around every four years. A house has to be a living thing—it should never be finished."

It was in 1969 that she started—with her friend Chessy Rayner—the decorating firm Mac II. "It sounds more like a trucking firm," she laughs. The Spartan sense of line and proportion, the crisp, the clean, the pellucid—the soothingly subdued are Mica's and Mac II's signature.

"My houses are very bare compared to most people's. I tend to tone down everything. I tried a couple of colors. Gray was my past—the last time I redid the house I changed the furniture from white to a silvery gray. This time I asked Chessy's opinion, she has a marvelous instinct for color, and then I ended up with white. It's the way I like to live. I love my objects and I want them to stand out." They do: the brass Regency palm trees, scrupulously fruited with coconuts, that hold sway in the living room; the Russian tea caddy found in a bazaar in Istanbul; the lemonade jar discovered in Paris and now used for an ice bucket; the nineteenth-century book trays, perfect for passing drinks.

"Color I like in carpets and paintings," she explains. Not that the Erteguns, who have been collecting for years—Mica is on the board of the Archives of American Art—view their pictures as wallpaper. If ever there is a house where art was a living force, this is it: Miró's *Amour,* Max Ernst's *Bird Who Sits and Does Not Sing,* Hockney's *Still Life on Glass-Topped Table,* Morris Louis's *Gamma Iota,* paintings by Gottlieb, Picabia, Clyfford Still, and Kenneth Noland, Magritte's *L'Empire des lumières,* diffusing its mysterious radiance in the living room, and, in the library,

Two views of the living room. Above: A fine 18th-century Russian secrétaire is flanked by two tables made by the 19th-century English painter Alma-Tadema. Opposite: An Ellsworth Kelly hangs across from a David Hockney, two Russian chairs sit under the palm trees, a late-18th-century Russian table serves the Biedermeier sofas.

an important collection of Russian Constructivist works.

When it came to redoing the third-floor library, Mica contemplated her modern glass bookshelves and "all the old books we had," then decided she wanted something that looked "not contemporary." "We were in the Dominican Republic one Christmas, at Oscar de la Renta's—they have the most beautiful mahogany in Santo Domingo and Oscar has this carpenter who is a genius. He built my bookcases there, from my design. They came here in two parts—I was petrified they wouldn't come up the staircase, but they just made it."

Two floors below, the kitchen was decidedly too small for the scale on which the Erteguns entertain (as often as not, thirty for dinner, with thirty more coming in afterward). Mica had it enlarged, but this took away from the existing dining room. Next, she had to enlarge the dining

room. "The house is narrow, so there was only one way to go—backward. Into the garden." *Mica* may mean small, but she certainly doesn't think small: to make the skylit enclosure—a two-story expanse of greenhouse/dining room—she used the same company that installed the Temple of Dendur for the Metropolitan Museum of Art. The walls of the enclosure are stucco "because this is kind of outdoors—and I like the texture." The floors are American stone, out of a quarry in the South. "I used to have black slate—too dark. This stone is uneven. Even the man who put it down for me said, 'Do you mind? It's light here, dark there.' But I *like* the fact that it's not all one color. It's also a very easy floor to maintain. Listen, we live in the twentieth century."

With that in mind, Mica reiterates her plea for the pure, uncluttered look. In one of the Erteguns' other two houses, a turn-of-the-century Victorian in Southamp-

ton, Long Island, "I have the same kind of concept I have in New York—simple, white—though we live in it in a different way; every place you go has its own tempo" and, in Ahmet Ertegun's native Turkey, in the small port of Bodrum, on the Aegean, the couple joined two old thick-walled stone fishermen's houses—lovingly restored, imaginatively added on to, and modernized—just a stone's throw from one of the seven wonders of the world, the Mausoleum of Halicarnassus. "Marble blocks and carvings have literally tumbled down into Mica and Ahmet's backyard," says a friend and frequent houseguest in Bodrum. Mica adds, "I did the house only with things you find in Turkey. I have banquettes and pillows. I consider it to be very Turkish but most Turks don't, I guess they don't like to live that way. Never mind—the house received the Aga Khan Award for Architecture." She confesses, "In Turkey, Ahmet and I argued a lot about

Preceding pages: *In the third-floor library a collection of Russian Constructivist works hangs above the fireplace. Part of the original fireplace, the antique frieze wittily refers to a mantel. Gilded dolphin-base table, behind sofa covered in fabric quilted in France, is English Regency.* Above: *A view past the David Smith sculpture on the left into the dining room, with its German Directoire chairs, to the garden beyond.* Right: *Ellsworth Kelly's* York, 1959, *hangs above the William IV table, which serves as a bar; Russian tankard stands in as an ice bucket.*

the decorating. In New York he just says, 'It's comfortable,' 'uncomfortable,' 'ugly,' or 'not ugly.' ''

Contrary to what one might expect, Mica, the decorator, gives Mica, her client, no preferential treatment. "It took me a year and a half to do the house in New York—it would have taken me eight months if I were someone else. When you do your own, you're the last one you get things done for. If I say to the upholsterer, 'Do my curtains,' and he has another client's to do, I say, 'Go ahead, do theirs first.' Also, if I'm looking for a special carpet for someone and I find it and then I see it would be perfect in my own living room, it goes to the client—I don't cheat."

And finally, is Mica her own most satisfied client? "Believe me, this is not the last time I'm going to do this house," she laughs, "but for now I am satisfied. After all, I can't demand more than what I have chosen for myself."

*Vincent Fourcade wanted
his house on Long Island,
here seen from the back,
to look "very American,
like a South Carolina
house," with a large
veranda.*

Vincent Fourcade

On the north side of the railroad tracks in the South Fork of Long Island, and in a rolling anonymous landscape that promises nothing in particular, is a house that has been lifted out of time, and out of place, and remade with an exuberant fancy. A house powered by memory, and by old affections still very much alive, it is also a tour de force of today's imaginings.

Unlike most houses built in the 1980s, it has a prehistory. Once, not so long ago, there was a very large house not an hour from Paris. It stood on the edge of the fôret de l'Île-Adam, with its prodigious oaks, its still unpolluted lakes and ponds, and its allées laid out by Le Nôtre. Built at the turn of the century, the house was furnished and decorated in the taste of the day—"faux Louis XVI–Ritz" on the one hand and Art Nouveau on the other. The Art Nouveau pieces—by Louis Majorelle, above all, but also by Eugène Vallin and others—were on an enormous scale, and custom-built for the house.

Among the children who spent much of World War II at this place, running free, bicycling, reading, swimming, absorbing their idiosyncratic surroundings in a world apart from the war, were the late Xavier Fourcade,

Above: *Watercolor of big living room by Janet Neff gets in more than the camera could capture.* Opposite: *Two-story main room has both the furniture and feeling of Fourcade's family's old house in France. Portrait at left,* La Belle Otéro, *is by an artist named Dannat; other portrait, by Mueller, is of Fourcade's grandmother as a young girl.*

who was to become an internationally known art dealer, and his younger brother Vincent, who is now (with his partner, Robert Denning) one of the most sought-after decorators in New York. They loved the house, and when the war was finally over and it could be put back into something approaching decent shape their father asked Xavier Fourcade to see what could be done. This father had his share of French thrift, and no great extravagance was encouraged. But Xavier even then was alert to every tremor of the market—he knew, for instance, that the forced closure of the great Parisian brothels had caused many an astonishing piece of Art Nouveau furniture to come on the market—and in contrast to the beiges and the pale honeys that had been mandatory in 1900 he used the bright and lively colors that were all the rage in the fifties. Gradually, the house came back to a double life, in which echoes of the heyday of Art Nouveau coexisted with high-keyed color.

Thus transformed, the house stayed in being till 1979, when the Fourcades' father died. The brothers were well established in New York, the rest of the family was widely scattered, their mother did not care to keep up the huge house by herself. Inevitably, it was sold. But what to do with the great custom-built Art Nouveau ensembles, and the additions that Xavier Fourcade had been able to make at almost laughable cost, and the tattered relics of earlier days that had been in trunks for thirty years?

For the Fourcade brothers, these things were their youth, their formation, their introduction to life. Vincent Fourcade by 1979 had a highly developed sense of what could be done with a house—*any* house—and above all of what could be done with the fundamentals of a house that in a real sense had been the making of him. Almost without hesitation he bought the contents of the house, and in 1980 he bought the land on Long Island on which his new house, named Monsoult, now stands.

He had no architect, no builder, and nothing specific in mind. What he did have was a lot of furniture that was too big, too strong, and too peculiar to take dictation. "I saw at once that the new house would have to be made to measure to fit the furniture, and also that I should need more of the same kind of thing to go with it. So Bob Denning and I went around New York, and to the auction sales. People who will pay anything for Tiffany lamps are frightened of the big set pieces, so we were able to buy quite well.

"Then I worked out the plan of the house. I wanted one enormous living room with a very high ceiling. It had to be living room, dining room, library, everything. I didn't know quite how to do it until I found out that [Karl

Above: *Looking beyond veranda to the gently rolling countryside. Door moldings by David Mills are the large-scale type usually used on exteriors.*
Opposite: *Mammoth double-sided chimney ascends to the ceiling from fireplaces framed with grotesque faces (inspired by Guimard house in Paris and Bomarzo Garden of Monsters outside Rome), sculpted in plaster by David Mills.*

Friedrich] Schinkel had designed a shooting lodge for Prince Antoine Radziwill that had a living room three stories high. In the middle of it was an immense double-sided fireplace with a flue that was like a great pillar. I saw that, and I said to myself that that was what would give the room its oddity—I think a room has to be odd—though, of course, I couldn't foresee quite what it would look like.

"When it was built, it looked like I had the flue of a factory in my living room with two openings at the bottom of it. How was I to dress it up? Well, I remembered how in great Art Nouveau houses like the Solvay house in Brussels they had varnished brickwork next to sophisticated paneling. So I decided to keep the patterned bricks of the big chimney quite bare, as if I had meant to do it all the time, and I had them painted with six coats of paint and then varnished, so that they looked like enameled tiles. But I still had the problem of the two openings. I needed something strange, but what? Then I remembered how Guimard had made doorways in the shape of monsters' heads with open mouths and how the Italians had done the same during the Renaissance in gardens like Bomarzo, and I decided to do the same. But how to do it? That was something else." The answer came when Vincent Fourcade happened upon the work of David Mills in a New York restaurant. Mills turned out to be a craftsman who loved plastering and loved Art Nouveau; he agreed to make the fireplace, and he and his sister spent every weekend working on it. "It all went perfectly," says Fourcade, "and he made two fantastic faces— two faces of very ugly people with wide open mouths.

"As the living room is really very big, I decided to give it unity by using a fabric that could go all the way up the walls and also go on the furniture. So I went to Le Manach and saw a wonderful damask, a sort of 1900 horse-chestnut-leaf pattern, that was just right, and I had it made up in chintz. You can make a terrible mistake and end up with a place looking like a zoo, but this one was not too heavy, and we had it made up with the same caramel background that I already had in the pieces of velvet salvaged from the portières of the house in France. In this way I could use both the velvet and the chintz on the same chair, if I wanted to, so that the feeling of the old house and the feeling of the new house became one.

"I took care to have some very big chairs and some very small ones, because in an enormous room changes of scale are important, and I also brought in a lot of sculptures as punctuation to offset the sweetness of the fabric. They are not very good sculptures, but they ricochet off one another. You have to be very skillful to make a big room

Left: *In the downstairs
bedroom panels from the
old family house are
cartoons for tapestries by
Jean Baptiste Huet, circa
1780.* Above: *Between
French bookcases, circa
1820, is a door from the
old house which
Vincent's brother, art
dealer Xavier Fourcade,
had made: the most
revered French authors
are matched up with the
slangy titles of a crime-
novel series.* Below:
*Lovers on the English
needlepoint rug,
alternately identified as
Romeo and Juliet and
Ivanhoe and friend, were
taken from a painting by
Paul Delaroche.*

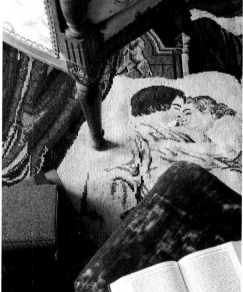

Above: *Fourcade says porch "is from all those books on Italian villas." Wainscoting was inspired by Russian film of* Anna Karenina. *Opposite above:* Majorelle *furniture in upstairs bedroom was originally bought for Fourcade's grandparents' bedroom. Opposite, below left: Other side of room shows fireplace, mantel, mirror, tiles from French house. Original painted velvet on chaise (and bed), formerly curtains. Opposite, below right: Hallway walls have stenciled pattern that partly creeps over panels of Greef lace.*

comfortable, and it has be be as comfortable when you are two or four as when you are twenty.

"As for the house in general, I did not want it to look like a transplanted French house that would act as a shock in the landscape. I wanted it to look very American from the outset, and very symmetrical. As I already had such firm ideas, and as I already had a very good contractor who was all set to go, it was not a very inviting job for an architect. But Steven Potter agreed to undertake the thankless task, and it is thanks to him that we now have the little hall with its stand for hats and coats and umbrellas and the pretty banquettes that I cut down from the ones in the pool room in France. He told me, and quite rightly, that people had to have somewhere to put down their things.

"My builder, Robert Hartwell, was quite extraordinary. I knew him very well, and we worked with him on every detail. A great piece of luck was finding that fantastic doorway that stands between the hall and the living room. It's so big that no one had ever dared to buy it, but in this house it's exactly right."

Upstairs and downstairs, a cosmopolitan fancy has been at work. The large areas of terrazzo flooring may have a bloom like that of the floors in a Roman villa, but they were inspired by the long-running, hard-wearing look of the terrazzo floors in River House in New York, and they were carried out by a team of second- or third-generation Italian craftsmen who drove out from Queens in a truck and arrived at six o'clock every morning.

But fundamentally this remains a family house, full of family things. Even the tiles around the tub in the downstairs bathroom were taken from an old window box in the French house. There are family portraits, family photographs, and family jokes, like the fake book bindings on a bedroom door connecting with a bathroom, for which Xavier Fourcade took the names of the great French writers—Bossuet, Racine, La Fontaine—and matched them with the titles of pulp thrillers of our own day. The present is very strong in this house, but the past is very strong, too. If it sounds like a Proustian adventure, that's exactly what it is. If there are also Chekhovian elements—well, it so happens that the name of the house near Paris was La Cerisaie (The Cherry Orchard). When the owners of the house come down for the weekend, with their station wagon full of potted flowers, they greet their surroundings in just the way that the owners of the doomed estate greet their beloved house in Act I of the great play. But the difference is that this particular cherry orchard will not be cut down, nor the Proustian overtones soon cease to be heard.

Suzie Frankfurt

Sumptuous trompe-l'oeil parquetry in Suzie Frankfurt's salon was painted by New York artisan Cile Lord after Russian originals, still the great pride of townhouses and palaces in the Soviet Union.

*I*n her New York town house, Suzie Frankfurt has assembled a set of rooms that evoke an unusual past—Russia of the 1820s and '30s, the age of Pushkin, the golden age of Russian literature. The origin of Frankfurt's chosen decoration is a bit unusual as well. "I used to think about Russia all the time," she says. "I'm from California, brought up on the beach at Malibu. I was fair and freckled easily and had to stay out of the sun, so I dreamt about snowy winters in Siberia." Out of those winter dreams has come a house of great dramatic flair, Romantic and Russian to the core. Its Russianness is exotic and exciting, too, in the middle of Manhattan. "Most people in New York are used to French and English furniture," Frankfurt says. "When I design rooms for them they ask me to use it; it feels *right* to them. If I were from the East, perhaps I'd feel that way too. But these monumental Russian things are somehow right to my California imagination. I like their strangeness."

The strangeness and sometimes austere formality and massiveness of Russian rooms is tempered everywhere in this house by Italian grace and elegance. The house rings right; its Russian references are strong and dramatic. "Of course, I was only in Russia once," Frankfurt smiles.

Left: *A 3rd-century Gandhara head in gray schist contemplates the salon between a pair of 19th-century gilded silver fruit dishes from Petersburg. Mirror of giltwood and beveled blue glass is 18th-century German. Andirons from William H. Jackson.*
Below left: *The ceiling of the salon mirrors the floor; its design is copied from another Russian parquet pattern. An 18th-century Russian inlaid sewing table stands in front of a Jacob settee covered in Clarence House fabric. The walls are glazed in the same green as a hall in the former Mikhailovsky Palace in Leningrad, now the Russian Museum.*
Opposite: *In the bedroom, Warhol's portrait of Suzie Frankfurt glances back at an early-19th-century Italian nécessaire in verre églomisé.*

"For four days. So this house is my own Russia. I made it up." The amazing thing is that a fantasy should correspond so closely to historical reality. For the splendid flowering of Russian decorative arts in the early decades of the nineteenth century was in fact the result of a hundred years of cross-fertilization with Italian architects and designers, many of whom settled in Russia and did their major work for the imperial courts. It was through these great architects and designers—Bartolomeo Rastrelli, Giacomo Quarenghi, Carlo Rossi, among others—that an Italian resonance became an indelible part of Petersburg, now Leningrad. The city itself became a kind of inverted mirror of Italy: Petersburg with its canals and palaces was called the Venice of the North. (The comparison is apt in summertime, when the city's architectural fantasies glimmer in the water, reflected through the milky light of the famous "white nights.")

A sense of this history forms a resonant background for Suzie Frankfurt's evocative rooms. The light shining through the windows onto the Italian pastel walls of the bedroom might be reflected off the Brenta Canal, the gleaming patterns of the parquets seem like extensions of Carlo Rossi's ballrooms, and the polished surfaces of exquisite wood grains reflect the elegances of Alexandrine Russia.

It is in the presence of wood surfaces above all that Russia makes itself felt. To this day the great glory of the Russian town houses and palaces are their parquet floors. "A friend gave me a book of designs and photographs of those floors," says Frankfurt. "I'd never seen anything so beautiful, and I wanted them everywhere. So I persuaded Cile Lord to try her hand at painting them for me. Before long we had transformed everything."

The furniture reflects the same presence of natural wood. Most eighteenth-century Russian pieces are copies of French or Italian designs, often painted. But at the turn of the nineteenth century, with the introduction of Empire and Restauration styles and the emphasis on natural woods, Russian cabinetmaking and furniture design came into their own. Russia is a land of forests, and wood is a native Russian element. The monuments of anonymous folk artisans and craftsmen, like the wooden Church of the Transfiguration at Kizhi, are unique in European art. With the introduction of Western models into Russia in the eighteenth century these craftsmen, most of them serfs, found a new challenge, and their talents gave an extraordinary dimension to the cabinetmaker's art. The Russians had, after all, an empire of their own, and enormous palaces to fill. The

*In the dining room, a
pair of Austrian
Biedermeier cabinets in
birchwood and an early-
19th-century Italian
bench in fruitwood and
gilt both have the
polished woods and
extraordinary curves the
Russians liked. The Belle
Epoque chandelier, 18th-
century giltwood mirror,
and Empire dining table
are all Italian.*

exaggerations they introduced into the international styles
of 1800 to 1830 were profoundly dramatic. Massive curves
appeared, as if the wood itself were dictating the style of the
piece, and polished expanses of matched burl and inlaid
woods reflected the the exquisite skill of craftsmen for
whom wood was a familiar and a loved presence.

But fine Russian pieces are comparatively
rare, not to be found everywhere. Much of Suzie Frankfurt's
furniture was bought in Italy, thus reinforcing the historical
connection: a charming Russian gueridon with carved mon-
key heads was found in Florence. And Italian furniture
styles, compared to the French, do have some Russian
strangeness—odd proportions, quirky touches of fantasy,
"like the furniture you see in your dreams," Frankfurt says.

No one, of course, knew better how rooms
could reflect our dreams than Russian writers like Pushkin,
Lermontov, and Gogol. They could easily have described
this house and felt at home here, perhaps have stretched out
to read during a long Russian night: every bed and sofa is
rich in pillows, and good lamps and books stand by in abun-
dance. And beneath the eaves is a real Russian *svetelka*, a
dormer room all done in red, a place to meditate while snow
falls beyond the small windows.

In the library, a pair of Russian chairs, circa 1820, are covered in a Clarence House striped satin. Throw pillows and curtains are all in antique fabrics. The great beechwood curve of its back identifies the Empire chaise as Russian, circa 1820. Amusing Regency table, also circa 1820, has faux camel legs. Secrétaire is Viennese Biedermeier.

"The ballroom scenes in Tolstoy and Pushkin—I wanted rooms like that," Frankfurt explains, and the salon is a skillful evocation of the charm of those rooms. The gleaming floors reflect muted daylight behind silk Austrian shades, while by night candles and crystal glitter overhead and fleeting reflections are caught between gilt frames in the antique mirrors that are the primary wall decorations. "A ballroom is all about reflections. The Russians understood that. The last scene in Balanchine's *Vienna Waltzes* is a perfectly Russian creation." The satin-covered borne is a quintessential ballroom adornment, and the walls are glazed the same green as the entrance hall of the former Mikhailovsky palace in Leningrad, now the Russian Museum.

"I suppose I wanted a stage set for my imagination," Suzie Frankfurt says. But she has created something more. Hers is a house permeated with a Romantic vision, and the vision is based on one of the great moments in the history of European design.

In the bedroom a French
flower chandelier hangs
over an 18th-century
Sicilian center table. A
pair of 18th-century
Italian giltwood mirrors
sets off a 17th-century
portrait of Petrarch's
inamorata Laura, in a
frame of the same period.
Chairs are Italian
Directoire, circa 1800, in
English antique fabric.

In the summer bedroom, as Grange calls it, neoclassical busts top gun pedestals that open for ammunition storage. Bronze horse on console is by Franz von Stuck. Overleaf: The library–dining room is an homage to the domestic atmospheres of Vuillard, with typically 19th-century Turkish carpets covering the furniture. Photograph-laden mahogany screen belonged to a 19th-century British horse-racing club.

Jacques Grange

*F*rench interior decorator Jacques Grange is a twentieth-century man living in a seventeenth-century Paris apartment with a distinctly nineteenth-century flavor. He is also an admitted romantic. He embraces his country's rich history, and has brought much of it alive in his own home. Everything about the apartment has a story that wants to be told, beginning with the apartment itself—the first floor of which was once home to the swashbuckling D'Artagnan and scene of his rendezvous with the beautiful Madame Bonacieux.

Grange himself first saw the apartment, which is on an easy-to-miss street near the Church of St. Sulpice, when he was fifteen and just beginning his education in the art of interior decoration at the Ecole Boulle. He entered the building through the street door, across the typical Parisian cobblestoned courtyard, up the narrow, winding stairway to the very top, which was then a painter's studio. Added to the building in 1925, the studio had an artist's secluded view of myriad Paris rooftops. Grange's first impression at his impressionable age was that he wanted to live there himself one day.

A few years later, Grange had finished his schooling at Paris's college of interior design, Ecole Camondo, begun his apprenticeship with an established deco-

Above: *The winter bedroom is furnished with a screen by Pierre Bonnard, a night table by Jacques Ruhlmann, a trompe-l'oeil velvet mushroom stool.* Opposite: *A window in the winter bedroom was cut to frame St. Sulpice.*

rator, and moved into the apartment he had set his heart upon. A couple years more, and he had charmed the elderly lady in the apartment below into selling him her place. And in time Jacques Grange had created rooms that remain cozily, comfortably, and unmistakably his very own. An expedition through this apartment is a delightful, unintimidating survey of centuries of artistic and decorative history—and a lesson in fearless and good-natured decorating. Generally nineteenth century, it is sparked with oddities from Louis XVI to Art Deco; pieces found over the years at favorite Parisian haunts—shops in St. Germain de Près, the Marché aux Puces—and during occasional sojourns in London.

From the beginning, Grange—who has his own business in Paris and is represented in New York by Didier Aaron, Inc.—decided his apartment asked for the cozy domesticity of a Vuillard painting. And indeed, the library/dining room is a space whose textures, colors, patterns, and details for contemplation would have had Vuillard himself poised with brush in hand: watercolor interior renderings sharing a terra-cotta mantelpiece with red candle screens painted by an unknown Cubist; Bavarian "corn dollies" for good luck on either side of the fireplace; a neo-Gothic lamp on a Biedermeier table; chairs and sofa and floor covered with thick Turkish and Kashmir carpets; and before it all, tea laid out with a simple flea-market tea set.

The upstairs "winter bedroom" has the same secure feeling: Kashmir and Egyptian carpets, a *table de malade* put to healthy use; photographs of preeminent artistic figures of the nineteenth century, taken by seminal photographers—Courbet and Bernhardt by Nadar, Baudelaire by

Below: In master bath, a pink flamingo ceramic mural from a turn-of-the-century Paris bistro. Sink was first a stove. Bottom: Guest room with added bath area has granite tub; floor is cement mixed with rose paint; bed is Empire. Right: Summer bedroom is furnished with table that was once Chateaubriand's, early-19th-century Russian screens of black wood and copper, Art Deco neo-grec chairs. Directoire iron bed.

Above: *Grange's studio, which he calls "Art Deco Colonial." Beige leather sofa by Pierre Chareau, stools by Jean Michel Frank used as cocktail tables, door handle by Ruhlmann.* Opposite: *Another view of winter bedroom with original fabric by Raoul Dufy, table by Polti, chair by Hoffmann.*

Carjat, Hugo, Verlaine—alongside engravings of exotic places like the Taj Mahal; a Goya engraving near a fake Picasso whose real counterpart is in the Hermitage.

Grange's playful juxtapositions also go farther back in history, to realize his vision for the "summer bedroom"—dusty-looking furniture, including flower chairs made for a winter garden; walls painted after the stone ones in Nohant, George Sand's country house.

The guest room is a "modern concept with a neoclassical atmosphere"—with its granite bathtub on a platform behind the splendid Empire bed; and then there is the studio and living room, where Jacques sometimes works, sometimes entertains, always has that view of Paris rooftops, along with his Art Deco piano, neo-Egyptian Liberty stool, and American Arts and Crafts rocking chair.

Obviously Jacques Grange feels that the character of "home" unfolds slowly, and that achieving it means using patience, optimism, and trust—letting your instincts lead you to the things that belong to you and letting affection put them all together.

Albert Hadley

*A*lbert Hadley, president of Parish-Hadley, which is to decorating what Mouton-Rothschild is to claret, says he's not a good houseguest. By which he doesn't mean to imply that he stays up all night and burns cigarette holes in the rug. To see Mr. Hadley—small, neat, gazing mildly at the world from behind round spectacles—is to know that's hardly his style. Rather, Mr. Hadley is the kind who likes to keep his own time, move at his own pace, and sleep in his own bed. That's why the place he bought near Tarrytown, New York, some years ago is a "godsend. I spent a lot of weekends in the city, working. But the house, once I got it, took over my life and everything else disappeared."

A farmhouse built about 1850 and sitting on a knoll, it wasn't at all what Mr. Hadley had in mind. "I'd always thought of having a much simpler, more classic box, perhaps on flat land. But here was this perfectly lovely house, so I couldn't resist.

"I remember every detail of seeing it and falling in love and thinking it an enormous challenge. No, an enormous *opportunity,* I should say, to do the things I like most—to create order and the atmosphere that I love." What is the atmosphere that Mr. Hadley loves? In three words: peaceful, private, precise.

Mr. Hadley's living room takes its elegance not from an overall decorating theory but from combinations of his favorite things, such as a hooked imitation-zebra rug, a wash drawing of an owl by Van Day Truex, and a 17th-century Dutch still life.

"I'm rather an orderly person and I don't like clutter. I like things, but I'm very interested in the juxtaposition of objects and the way materials look together. I love the excitement of discovery, but I'm not a collector. What I have, I have, and if I didn't have it I'd be happy with much less."

Soon after Mr. Hadley moved in "and got the land in better order" (order is clearly Mr. Hadley's favorite noun), he decided that the house needed a wider porch. He added one, with steps leading to a flagstone terrace; other than that, there was little to do but rebuild the chimneys.

"Inside was no problem at all. I had the furniture—some in storage, some I'd let people borrow, some family things I brought up from Tennessee—and I chose to keep everything as simple as possible." The house is white from top to bottom; some floors were sanded, cleaned, and left natural; those that weren't were painted dark green. Plain white muslin skirts the bottom half of each window because Mr. Hadley didn't want to impede the light and air and because he isn't too fond of curtains anyway. "Perhaps I shouldn't say that," he murmurs.

An ordinary weekend starts Friday afternoon when Mr. Hadley goes up alone to work the house's several acres. He loves to work outside but he is not, he says emphatically, a flower gardener. "I like ferns and such." Entertaining is mostly Saturday or Sunday lunch, usually on the porch. "I'm not awfully domestic. I manage a bit but it's not my great passion."

If by "domestic" Mr. Hadley means being a dab hand with a dustcloth and bread dough, he probably doesn't deserve the adjective. On the other hand, he's been fascinated by things pertaining to the home all his life.

Albert Hadley grew up near Nashville on farmland that had belonged to his grandfather, in a house that was built by his parents. They had very few neighbors in the beginning and he resented, he says, every new house that went up. That may be why, when he's describing the joy he takes in his farmhouse, several words keep repeating themselves: "the privacy...the isolation." His parents were interested in furniture—his mother was a collector— and he himself was "always interested in fashion, how tables were set, what people wore." He might have trained as an architect, "but at the time I thought it was too much engineering, too much mathematics and all the things I'm not exactly..." Instead, after the army, he went to New York and Parsons School of Design. He was there for four years and stayed on to teach; eventually, in 1962, he went

A gallery of Hadley vignettes. Top row, from left: English scroll table beneath reproduction of Irish plaster bas-relief (Sybil Connolly's gift); early painting by Mr. Hadley over English trolley table with original Tiffany-design lamps. Center: Early French oak table surrounded by English Regency chairs; French Deco pedestal urn below 20th-century American mirror. Bottom: 18th-century Portuguese table, bird drawing by Dudley Huppler; view from back porch of terrace and 19th-century urn.

to work with Sister Parish, whose partner he is still.

Given Mr. Hadley's travels in the realms of gold it is pleasant to hear that he found several of his own treasures by beating the Sanitation Department to a pickup. "The writing table with the blue cloth top I found on the street, and the tables by the beds in two of the guest rooms. And once [Mr. Hadley is visibly warming to his subject] I was walking on an uptown street, saw a glimmer of gold in the trash, and out came this *beautiful* Regency gilt bracket." Finding a Chippendale sofa just before it was to be turned into landfill was especially memorable. After being recovered it was "*wonderful.*"

Mr. Hadley is not only lucky in his walks, he is lucky in his friends, many of whom seem to spend a lot of time saying, "Ooh, just the thing for Albert." (Sister Parish's finding "just the thing for Albert" is how he acquired his farmhouse: she steered him to it.) He has a closetful of such things, and what he doesn't use he passes on. "There's a certain life about objects, I think, and the life goes on and on." A copper tray and candlestick, though, will stay forever. His mother gave them to him many years ago, saying, "I

bought these just for you." So will two circus drawings from a series by Byron Browne. The first he bought; Van Day Truex, the president of Parsons and his mentor, gave him its mate. "I couldn't have had a better present."

Mr. Hadley's best present to his friends and clients is, of course, his taste. "Tell me," asks a visitor, thinking to get a few tips, "do you have any one set of rules to design by?"

"Well," he replies, "I respect enormously the time and place of any architecture, and how one furnishes it depends on what it says. "Also, there's a continu-

Above: *In dining room, French 18th-century armchairs, 1860s English mahogany table, gilded ceramic gourd by Mrs. Hugh Hyde. Iron bookcases by Parish-Hadley. Right: Hadley uses porch "from spring until snow." Deer head above Aiken sofa is carved wood.*

Above: *Doors open opposite ways to two bedrooms off second-floor hall. Amusing 19th-century English chair is one of four. Initials <u>AH</u> inscribe chair's backrest. Left: A 19th-century "fainting couch" in a sunny living room corner.*

ity to one's taste. If you really like things they all tend to be of the same spirit and they all work together."

"If you have to *brood* about something, then," his visitor says, remembering a mirror framed in wood painted with wildflowers and a bird in flight and possibly still in residence at an antiques shop, "maybe you shouldn't get it?"

"If you don't know right away that something is something you want or can use," Mr. Hadley answers firmly, "you shouldn't buy it."

Ah, mirror, farewell.

William Hodgins

The living room seating focuses on the fireplace and water view through French doors. William Hodgins replaced an "unfortunate" mantelpiece with a 17th-century French one made of stone. One of several casual still lifes in the room is arranged on an old repainted desk and includes a serpentine stone ball on pedestal, an 18th-century Italian painted obelisk, and a pair of French bronzes.

I have never been so taken with a place," William Hodgins says of his Massachusetts North Shore house. "If I miss a weekend, I feel deprived." The Canadian-born decorator, who trained in New York at the Parsons School of Design and then with Sister Parish, has been successfully based in Boston since 1968. Like many professionals who are much in demand, he seeks weekend solitude. He managed to find a secluded property in a populated estate enclave in Manchester-by-the-Sea, one that faces a quiet saltwater cove and is reached by a lane that winds enough to discourage the approach of curious strangers.

The building was originally a carriage house, vintage last-quarter nineteenth century; the track from which huge sliding doors once hung is still visible on the outside. In the 1930s a family expanded the building as their residence and, to save fuel, dropped the ceilings to seven and a half feet. Hodgins, six feet six inches tall, was elated when he discovered he could raise the room height to well over nine feet. He also opened the space laterally, adding, where there had only been a small picture window, three large pairs of French doors facing the cove and opening to a generous new deck.

An acknowledged master of the pale, neutral palette, Bill Hodgins naturally colored his own retreat in the tones he likes best. His goal was a setting that would be "clean, cool, clarified, gentle." The designer smiles when he hears a British counterpart's color range described as "off-white to further off-white," noting that his

The spacious entrance
hall doubles as a setting
for occasional dinner
parties. Ordinarily the
old French table,
decorated by furniture
painter John Anderson,
stands against the
bookcase in which
creamware is displayed.
Hodgins accumulated six
similar Italian country
chairs, three seen here.
Floor painted by
Franklin Tartaglione.

Left: Stained glass oculus found in a flea market was placed in the wall of a new bathroom for the second guest room. Host Hodgins's rule: a bath for every bedroom. French chest of drawers is one of a handful of unpainted pieces in the house.
Below left: In the master bedroom, on the main floor, the large urn is one of several garden vessels and sculptures the designer likes to use indoors.

own boundaries are wider: "from stone to chalk perhaps." To the Hodgins office and its craftsmen, "old-world white" is shorthand not only for creamy, soft, old-looking color but also, says an associate, "for a state of mind."

One of the advantages of an old-world white milieu, the designer points out, is that the eye can concentrate on shapes, for "with white you aren't hiding anything." At the Hodgins house this means savoring rounded antique tables and chairs (Italian and French, painted and unpainted), small bronzes and other objects, a collection of creamware, a subtly painted checkerboard floor. And it means weekends not only of solitude but of a quiet appreciation of home.

*Although he enjoys
solitude, William
Hodgins sometimes fills
his two upstairs guest
rooms. Under the eaves
is the 'ladies' favorite''
with its window seat and
tiny operable eyebrow
window. Early-19th-
century English brass bed
has unusual upholstered
headboard.*

John Maurer

As a designer, John Maurer worked for years among "lots of glitz"; a house in the country—in his case the area around Roxbury, Connecticut—provided a refuge from all that. His dream was to escape permanently. "Everyone talks about it—all the weekenders," he says. "But one day I said to myself, 'Either you're going to talk about it for the rest of your life or you're going to do it.' I realized I'd rather fox hunt on Tuesday than go to the D & D building."

If the Decoration & Design building he refers to stands for the life he has left behind in New York, fox hunting, under the auspices of the Fairfield County Hunt, represents the life he has found. Indeed, the hunt was the area's chief attraction for him when he first moved there. In the years that followed, an influx of new residents drove up real-estate values dramatically, and Maurer rode the market's crest, fixing up and "trading up" houses twice. Then, once his career was Connecticut-based, he took to buying houses and fixing them up for others, and this he still does. For himself, however, he wants nothing more than what he calls his "cozy cottage."

Tall, he has a slight stoop that may have come from adapting himself to the proportions of this, his

Above: *A pencil-post Shaker bed hung with lace furnishes the master bedroom.* Opposite: *The dining room was left unelectrified "to force the use of candles." Staffordshire china sets a circa-1750 Connecticut gate-leg table in the style of William and Mary and fills an actual English William and Mary "Welsh" cupboard. A Canton plate stands alone on a plate rack. Curtains, Clarence House.*

third house. Built in 1720, it had changed hands only once before, in the nineteenth century. The generations of farmers who had lived here never had the means to make major alterations. A few taps at the Masonite walls revealed old plaster behind, and the original wide floorboards lay beneath the linoleum. So warped were the latter, however, that they had to be removed, waterblasted, and then relaid. To provide room for insulation, a new roof was built out over the existing one. In all, the structural work took over a year, costing, Maurer estimates, twice what a new house would have—not that he ever considered that alternative. "I love the crooked corners of old houses," he says. "They even smell old."

Despite his respect for the original structure of the house, Maurer sought to avoid a pedantically "correct" décor. True, there are good American pieces—like a tea table in the living room and a gate-leg table in the dining room—that happen to be of the precise period and locality as the house. In general, however, the Puritanical strictures of unalloyed eighteenth-century Americana have been ignored, while visual non sequiturs—involving a telling mix of times and places—have been encouraged. A bit of Beatrix Potter here, a bit of John Fowler at home in the country there (in such details as antique needlepoint bell-pulls used to give the impression of greater height to low ceilings)...all of these suggest a more than passing acquaintance with Albion.

In fact, Maurer will say, he is English on his mother's side, and he visited the British Isles every summer as a child. His interest in fox hunting comes from a grandfather who raised thoroughbreds in County Cork; perhaps the earliest inspiration for this house was a cottage belonging to his great-grandmother in Stratford-upon-Avon. The famous Elizabethan knot gardens there made a particularly deep impression on him, which he was finally able to recreate in Roxbury. Out of fashion by 1720 in England, this wonderfully artificial arrangement of lavender, santolina, and box might well have been found in the Colonies at this point—but probably not beside so simple a farmhouse.

"The original garden," Maurer allows, "must have been less formal and more practical." Similarly, within, although the walnut paneling in both the living and dining rooms is of the exact period as the house, its high style might make one question its authenticity. "The romance, of course, would have been that I found it underneath everything," Maurer says. "Actually, there were only typical nothing farmhouse mantelpieces. I bought the paneling from a dealer who specializes in old lumber."

Above left: *A view of the living room shows walnut paneling not original to the house but of its precise period.* Above right: *Another living room corner, with Schumacher-fabric swags at the windows.* Opposite: *Old floorboards were removed, waterblasted, and relaid. The 19th-century hooked rugs have unusual linen backings. A Connecticut tea table, circa 1720, bears its original finish.*

For all these fancy touches, there is no feeling here of excess. What seems most particularly English about this house is the legerdemain with which Maurer has simultaneously ennobled the humble and humbled the noble. In the dining room he has combined the unpretentious Staffordshire he loves with a fine Canton plate; in the living room two Canton jars, placed on Adamesque brackets "much too good to be here," complement smart Federal-style curtains, some Victorian near-kitsch, and a simple antique bootblack's box "that's nothing. But I think it all works well together.

"And you just love it, don't you?" Maurer asks, addressing a pair of bearded collies with whom he shares the house. Their breed guarantees the dog hairs that are a final, requisite component of the look he has evoked. "They're *encouraged* to climb all over everything," he says.

Apart from the dogs, his greatest passion is the hunt that brought him here in the first place. "I'm five minutes from the stables," he points out. "I love it not just for the sport of it but for the pageantry. Everybody's all gussied up and flying across the fields and in the fall the leaves are turning. Then in the wintertime when you go out it's still dark. There are mornings when the mist is coming out of the earth and a sunbeam will come through the trees...it's incredible. You'd never see anything like it if you weren't out on a horse at that time of day. At times like that, New York seems *very* far away."

Juan Pablo Molyneux

Juan Pablo Molyneux's Buenos Aires pied-à-terre is an apartment of many moods entered through a bare, gleaming foyer with marble floor and lacquered walls. Pine column is contemporary; German caryatid bracket is old.

*T*he entry is white and bare, the library is dark and velvety, the dining room is hard and glittering. "I like defined spaces," the apartment's owner and designer, Juan Pablo Molyneux, explains, "even in a place that is small."

When the Chilean-born designer decided to live and work in New York as well as Buenos Aires, he and his wife, Pilar, moved from their vast apartment in Buenos Aires to a pied-à-terre in an old French-style building in that city's most fashionable neighborhood.

The neighborhood was one of the apartment's attractions, and so was the height of the rooms. Another advantage turned out to be the very poor condition of the existing interior surfaces, which Molyneux felt gave him license to tear down every room partition and build anew.

Within the empty shell, the designer developed a completely different floor plan and enriched it with luxurious decorative detail. He paved his front rooms with white marble, coffered two of the ceilings in Renaissance style, and topped all the major doorways with traditional arches, which frame interior vistas. Another bit of indoor scenery-making was the conversion of an outside balcony into a greenhouse viewed from several rooms.

Molyneux's broad taste, unified by a preference for the formal, spans many centuries and draws upon many styles. With this stock in trade, it is little wonder that his practice spans two continents.

Left: *On living room walls, a tiny-patterned fabric designed by Molyneux. Also his design: the seating, the marble-and-Lucite coffee table. Overleaf, left: The designer enlarged his tiny dining room, whose 4-by- 4-foot hexagonal mahogany table almost fills it, by making it "a mirrored box" with a strict no-color palette. Regency chairs are lacquered and gilded. Paintings are 16th- century Dutch; chandelier is English. Overleaf, right: Dark brown velvet walls, red-and-gold coffered ceiling, Persian rugs give the library its own strong character. Molyneux achieved this long view within a small area.*

Renzo Mongiardino

I'm not a decorator," says Mongiardino, "I'm a creator of ambience, a scene designer, an architect, but *not* a decorator." Coming as it does from the begetter of some of today's most ornate interiors, this claim might well puzzle people who have not had the good fortune to visit Mongiardino's Milanese apartment. For its deliberately *délabré* patina and nostalgic air would suggest that nothing has changed since the end of the last century. Who indeed could blame a casual visitor for assuming that the present occupant had inherited the apartment—lock, stock, and barrel—not from his parents but from his grandparents and that a visit from a decorator was, if anything, overdue?

In fact Mongiardino bought the apartment, gutted it, and, in his capacity as an architect, totally remodeled it. Except for a few modest heirlooms, virtually everything is fake—contrived by the owner. But so cunningly has it all been done that the eye no less than the mind is fooled into perceiving the apartment as a miraculous *ottocento* survival—cultivated rooms that evoke the period of the *Macchiaioli* painters. In the circumstances, Mongiardino is quite right to describe himself as "a creator of ambience." Therein lies his artistry.

Preceding pages and right: *In one of two studios in Mongiardino's apartment, samples of tiles, bits of marble, verre églomisé, reliquaries, interior renderings by two of his collaborators, and 19th-century engravings of furniture and pelmets adorn the walls.*

By way of explanation Mongiardino says that
he wanted to re-create the atmosphere of his parents' handsome *palazzo*. He has certainly succeeded in manipulating
the time warp, wafting the visitor back, in imagination, to
the illustrious circle of Manzoni, Boito, and Verdi. Mongiardino himself enhances this illusion: with his abundant whis-
kers he actually resembles Verdi in middle years; he has the
same blend of authority and geniality and a grand manner
that is all the more attractive for being without artistic pre-
tensions or fashionable airs. No wonder one merchant
prince after another—Agnelli, Heinz, Niarchos, Rothschild, Thyssen, to name but a few—has put himself and his
treasures into these gifted hands.

Deceit is Mongiardino's secret weapon. In
this respect his work puts one in mind of Degas's astute observation: "A picture is something that requires as much
cunning, trickery, and deceit as the perpetration of a crime."
One feels that Mongiardino would rather paint wood to
look like wood than have to contend with real appearances.
A case in point is the set of large bookcases in the main salon:
the kind of neoclassical furniture favored by early-nineteenth-century cognoscenti. What could be more authentic
looking? But—trust (or should one say don't trust?) Mon-

giardino—these bookcases turn out to have been conjured
out of deal which assistants have stained and painted and patinated. Thanks to Mongiardino's instinctive understanding
of scale and texture and the minutiae of style, his pastiches
look more real than the real thing. The same goes for the
"eighteenth-century" busts that adorn these "antiques";
they turn out have been executed far more recently than two
hundred years ago. Don't however, attribute this passion for
illusion to some kind of hang-up but rather to a preoccupation with the overall aesthetic effect, at the expense (so far as
his own apartment is concerned) of museum standards of
authenticity or quality!

Working as he does for some of the world's
most prestigious collectors, Mongiardino is a past master at
displaying his clients' treasures. But for his own surroundings he evidently prefers furniture that evokes a mood or enhances an ensemble to signed pieces that smack of period
pedantry. Take, for instance, the set of well-worn leather
furniture that surrounds the fireplace in the big room—furniture that Mongiardino's parents bought in London short-
ly before the First World War. Hardly the sort of thing one
would find in the window of Mallet's or Aveline, but how
perfectly its faded Edwardian swagger—shades of Lutyens

and Elgar—harmonizes with the faded Italian swagger that characterizes Mongiardino's settings for himself. And how characteristic of a man who admits to preferring things that are the worse for wear, to complete this ensemble with a pouf contrived out of matching reddish leather—leather that has been distressed in the same degree and then appliquéd with a facsimile of the rusty patchwork that we find in the curtains (authentically old ones—from a grandmother). And again how characteristic of Mongiardino *not* to smarten up his parental chairs with a barrage of cushions that "make a statement." Far from gilding the lily, as he did to such good effect at the Rothschilds' Hôtel Lambert, the maestro has been at pains in his own quarters to play things down. Hence all the contrivance that has been lavished on making things look the reverse of contrived.

Whereas most decorators with a fashionable following endeavor to keep the not-so-raw materials of their trade from contaminating their private apartments, Mongiardino makes no bones about wallowing in his work. Evidence of this is everywhere. Samples of stuffs are as likely to be found by a drink tray or on a bedside table as by a drawing board. By the same token the big room has not been devised as a salon for entertaining so much as a study in which to discuss projects and pore over albums and portfolios. Stacks of these cover the surface of the vast table which takes up more than half the area of this vast room—a room that evokes the eighteenth-century rationalism of a *cabinet d'amateur* while also hinting at the nineteenth-century fantasy of Spalanzani's gallery in the *Tales of Hoffman.*

When questioned about the pride he takes in his métier, Mongiardino's enthusiasm never fails him. He sees art in terms of craft, the past in terms of the present, and declares that his dream is to live in a large house where he and his colleagues can work together on all manner of decorative projects, on the revival of dead or dying crafts as well as on the development of new techniques. "Like a medieval guild," says Mongiardino, who regards everything he does, even his own apartment, as "a joint effort for which all must share the credit." This idealism, this lack of worldliness or egotism is closer in spirit to William Morris's Kelmscott than the Decorators' Building.

"*Luxe, calme et fantaisie*"—to misquote Baudelaire—would seem to be the keynote of Mongiardino's work. If in his apartment the emphasis is more on the *calme* than the *luxe*, this can be attributed to the maestro's dislike of self-promotion or pampering. He has aimed at devising a far from luxurious décor that matches his reclusive-poetic temperament rather than one that would advertise

Opposite above: *In salon, Mongiardino designed the bookcases and moldings around ceiling. All furnishings and decorative elements are pastiches made to his design, except patchwork curtains from his grandmother's house.* Opposite below: *In master bedroom, blue damask wallpaper found in Genoa sets off a 19th-century Genoese portrait over bed draped in red velvet. Gouaches over bedside table by Lila de Nobili. Mongiardino designed the bookcase.* Above: *In front hall, obelisk designed by Mongiardino in front of 17th-century painting from the palazzo where he grew up.*

his skills or serve as a vitrine for his wares. This approach is evident in the master bedroom, which is fastidious without being precious—what Berenson called "life-enhancing" without being eye-catching. Note the bold use of a damask-patterned wallpaper of an intense gentian blue. This blue—so difficult to use that cautious designers traditionally fight shy of it—holds the disparate elements of the room together besides engendering a celestial, Ingresque light.

And how touching the guest room is in its simplicity and, that rare quality, family piety. Presided over by a bravura portrait of the maestro's beautiful mother is the suite of 1880s-ish furniture that graced his parents' bedroom. Although big (and, by today's standards, ugly) for the space into which it has been squeezed, this suite "goes" wonderfully well, thanks largely to the way walls, beds, and chairs are covered with the same nineteenth-century floral linen made by Rubelli—a busy little pattern such as Vuillard loved to paint. Bath after bath of tea has given this stuff a look that can only be described as Jamesian—a look that Visconti might have evoked if he had ever filmed *The Portrait of a Lady*.

His theatrical sense enables Mongiardino to evoke a wealth of atmosphere. Just as a stage designer immerses himself in the atmosphere of a play, Mongiardino immerses himself not just in the architectural nature of the house or apartment he has been commissioned to embellish but in the personality of the clients and the atmosphere they generate around them. In each case the atmosphere is of course very different; hence the variety that is such a feature of Mongiardino's work. As for his own apartment, the *Stimmung* that Mongiardino has evoked is so attractive, so palpable that one is tempted to export slabs of it to this side of the Atlantic where it might humanize some of our bleaker "*Bauhaüser*."

Apropos the international movement, one can't help wondering about Mongiardino's rapports with Milan's uncompromisingly contemporary designers. "They used to criticize me," he wryly admits, "for the solecism of using columns. But now many designers are using columns themselves, so they can no longer take that line. And so I may be obliged to move onto something else." What an irony that his traditionalism and nostalgia should have put Mongiardino ahead of the game.

Above: Guest room is furnished with a suite from Mongiardino's parents' Genoa palazzo. Walls and bed covered in a Rubelli fabric. Boldini-style portrait of Mongiardino's mother is by Maggi, a Turin painter. Opposite: In another view of front hall, objects mix with Empire stool in architectural setting of stucco masonry and trompe-l'oeil coffered ceiling.

Sister Parish

*T*hey all ask me the same question," says Sister Parish. She
speaks in a low, you might say tentative, voice, but nothing
she says is tentative. "They all ask me, 'How did you get into
this?'" A dull question, she implies.

"This" is the business of making other peo-
ple's houses attractive, an art as well as a business at which
Sister Parish preeminently excels, and has excelled for quite
a long time. Back in the early 1930s, the Harry Parishes were
a newly married couple, and though living in the shadow of
the Depression, they owned pretty things. Sister's parents
had footholds in New York and Paris; she grew up in fine
rooms finely set out. "I had no formal education," she says.
"I just had my natural instincts to rely on. I was never a
scholar like John Fowler." She resembled in many ways a
London counterpart, Lady Colefax, who, also in the Depression years, turned a gift for creating warm and welcoming interiors into a vocation.

Almost imperceptibly Sister Parish began to
distribute her own likings among her friends, until today she
has created for herself an exemplary position as arbiter of
taste, as counselor, as inspiration for a faithful roster of clients and disciples. Partly she has done this by force of character. She has perfected a lifetime habit of getting to know

Another view of the
living room, where a
portrait of Sister Parish
hangs over the mantel,
with painted bronze dogs,
enamel candlesticks, and
old prints; on the left a
late-18th-century
girandole. Hand-painted
silk-and-velvet pillows
carry through the floral
motif on a sofa covered
in Scalamandré damask.
Behind is an English
18th-century mirror that
belonged to her family.
The carpet is Aubusson.

Above: *In the library a French screen showing a cage and various birds stands behind a painted Italian table with a Chinese decoupage vase lamp and a book about a peke called* Wee Jade Button. *Opposite: Also in the library is an 18th-century English secretary filled with ivory objects and a Chippendale chair covered in needlepoint.*

and understand those who seek her help. She crystallizes their impulses and nourishes their understanding.

Her most recent apartment, on Fifth Avenue and once the home of Gloria Swanson, shows how her talent works when it is given free rein. It is an apartment at street level, with a paved courtyard garden in which the tutelary deities of the house, her two pekes, Nanni and Henryk (named after a favorite client, Henryk de Kwiatkowski), can take the air. "I didn't buy anything new," she says, "I just used what I have. Everything here has a meaning for me. It belonged to my father, like that desk. Or Harry and I found it in a French château. Or it reminds me of a friend. Or I found it amusing. You don't need to go shopping. You make do with what you have."

Admittedly this is easier if you already possess ravishing objects—some of the first order, some content to be merely ravishing—and if you know how to display them. Ivories are strewn on flat surfaces, and polished wooden boxes—a glowing apple, say—nestle against a tortoiseshell birdcage. On three walls hang large and vivid chi-

Left: *In her very feminine bedroom Sister Parish used chintz from Sanderson for curtains, armchair, bed trim; bedspread chintz from Cowtan & Tout. In front of oval Adam mirror is a bust of Sister. Above bed is a tin candle bracket with porcelain flowers. Below left: Fantasy chinoiserie painted panels from Philippe Farley hang in the library. Table covered in a fabric from Clarence House, chairs around the table covered in Cowtan & Tout chintz, and armchairs in a Brunschwig glazed chintz. Custom-painted sisal carpet is from Patterson, Flynn & Martin.*

noiserie panels on canvas taken from a house in Provence. Sister Parish has a special gift for plump, brilliant, tempting pillows so that it is hard to pass one of her chairs without sinking into it. And she is an adept at swags and pelmets. Where other designers often suffocate a room in sheer excess of fabric, her effects, if rich, are also light.

It is commonplace to say her taste is based on English models. Certainly she has been a lifelong friend of English designers such as Sybil Colefax and Nancy Lancaster, but in reality all that she shares with such colleagues is a luminous sense of comfort and color. True, there is effectively no such thing as a specific English taste. Unlike French or Italian or German houses, the better houses of Britain seldom (and until the 1930s almost never) have been tamed by experts. They just grew around their owners, who might or might not match an acquisitive sense with a sense of decorum.

But Sister Parish, like the best of her European contemporaries, is a creator of harmonies. Her chintzes set off the flowers that are everywhere, and both are scaled to human use and relaxation. She does not aim to create a Brideshead, to evoke a gasp, but to fit livable rooms to those who live in them.

Because people are different, her houses are different, too. Moreover, she is usually right in her judgments for her clients, they confess. She does not bully them, she overrides their objections and in the end compels them to be grateful. She is an infectious teacher, too. After a few years of working with Sister Parish, many Americans have earned a niche for themselves in art history by becoming truly expert as collectors. Starting out, perhaps, without an excess of knowledge or interest, they have succumbed to her enthusiasm and become enthralled by the possibilities of study. There is nothing dry about Sister Parish's scholarship. She plays it down perhaps, but it backs her every design.

It is assumed that the principles of modern decoration rest very largely on the work of Edith Wharton and Ogden Codman, laid out in *The Decoration of Houses*. In the nineteenth century a room was admired too often because it was crowded and expensive: palms in Japanese pots, Fabergé fancies, and extravagant pieces of sculpture with titles like *Puck on a Toadstool*. Later, simplicity took over. This was an aesthetic improvement certainly but seldom a source of practical pleasure: no chairs were ever less comfortable than the now much-admired chairs of Charles Rennie Mackintosh, for one thing. French paneled rooms and the white furnishings of Syrie Maugham took the world by storm. But it was Sister Parish who first perfected the art of the inviting. Her rooms beckon to the beholder.

Mrs. Parish has a country home in Dark Harbor, Maine, and here one of the sources of her inspiration becomes plain. She brings the country to the city, for it is evident that she is at heart a country person. She can be as grand as anybody, but she is most at home in a world of flowers and summer delights. Fifth Avenue is not meadowlike, nor by its nature serene. But right there in her little paved yard, with its impatiens gleaming in a shady corner, she has transplanted a touch of country living to an apartment for which inviting is the word.

John Saladino

*A*t the lowest point of New York City's mid-1970s fiscal and spiritual slump, the John Saladino family expressed their faith in the rebirth of the city by acquiring a portion of railroad robber-baron Jay Gould's vast triplex apartment, including its properly baronial ballroom. The apartment as we see it today incorporates a synthesis of John Saladino's life in design with elements expressing his architectural and historical interests and the family's heritage.

Two constants in John Saladino's work from his earliest "minimalist" days have been a sense of the subtle interaction of color with light and an absolute fanaticism about the quality of workmanship. In this apartment the flow of light and repetition of colors and textures unify the rooms despite their widely varying sizes. A large contingent of artist-craftsmen produced first-rate work in response to the designer's passionate desire for technical perfection.

John Saladino describes his apartment on one level as a "space-time continuum." He had a definite progression in mind when planning the rooms. The visitor arrives first, of course, in the elevator hall, known as the *caldarium*, after the hottest room in an ancient Roman bath. Like all elevator halls, it is in fact warm. The elevator doors have been painted by artist David Fisch (who did most of the trompe l'oeil, textured painting, and metal leafing in the apartment) to resemble the coffered bronze doors of an ancient temple like the Pantheon. The walls are stonework in paint enlivened with carved swags—three real, one painted.

In John Saladino's Manhattan apartment, vaulted ceiling, fountain, and trompe-l'oeil elevator door transform entry into room from a Roman bath. Overleaf: Doric column marks center of foyer dining room.

Water splashes from an eighteenth-century French porphyry lion's-head fountain, reinforcing the impression of an entrance courtyard in some Mediterranean country. Overhead, a newly installed vaulted ceiling is decorated with charming figures in Pompeian style that close friends will recognize as astrological representations of the Saladino family.

From this anteroom, the visitor steps into the oval foyer of the apartment itself. The owner refers to it as the *mastaba,* after an ancient Egyptian tomb type that was built exactly like a house of the period so the resident spirit would feel comfortably at home. This area is the heart of the apartment; even the bleached oak floorboards which run through every room are laid so they center here. Nearly all the colors, textures, and shapes used in the entire apartment appear in this area as a kind of preview of coming attractions. A windowless interior space, it is given a sense of light and height by a highly lacquered oval ceiling dome. The lofty-appearing dome is in reality only three inches deep, the technical tour de force of the apartment, according to project manager John Nihoul, whose fiendishly demanding job

included overseeing the day-to-day construction. The foyer walls are partly plastered with the roughest of undercoats, partly paneled with super-smooth brushed metal.

The epicenter of the foyer and of the entire apartment is the freestanding Doric column whose unfinished plaster fluting masks a supporting beam while relating in style to both the Roman anteroom and the Italianate living room yet to come. The column and the ceiling vault are both cleft, because John Saladino wants the apartment to have the atmosphere of a "civilized ruin," a fragment of some larger complex. The cleft in the column is filled with oxidized copper, that in the ceiling with lights. An Adam-style carved pine doorway salvaged from a stately home in Norfolk, England, prepares the visitor for the scale and grandeur of the living room on the other side.

It's an orchestrated shock to step through from the enclosed dimly lit *mastaba* to the enormous drawing room, so flooded with light and air that you might be out of doors. Glass doors straight ahead seem to hint at a garden beyond, though in fact they open onto small balconies far above the busy street. North and south light pours in through three vast windows with bottom sills set well above normal ceiling height. In order not to block the light, they are covered only by gossamer shades of a Groundworks material called, fittingly, *"opalin cristal"* — "a dragonfly's wing," according to the owner/designer. At night their iridescence gently reflects the room's lighting.

The erstwhile ballroom is 23 feet wide by 35 feet long with 23-foot ceilings. It is nearly a double cube, a proportion that has been considered since classical times to impart a feeling of stability and calm. Everything in the room is scaled to its size. It is a kind of a fantasy setting where almost all the furnishings are gigantic but appear quite normal. The seventeenth-century Italian refectory table, for instance, is a piece of walnut thirteen feet long, fully adequate to feed all the inhabitants of a medium-sized monastery at once. Traffic on the street below was stopped while the table was hoisted into place because the building's service elevator is not nearly large enough to accommodate such a slab. Sofa backs are four feet high. These chairs are so exaggerated in their size and the angle of their backs that John Saladino, who found them gathering dust at Didier

Aaron in Paris, is convinced they must have been theatrical props whose back legs were made short to appear upright on steeply raked stages. Enormous cushions cluster on the sofas; the marble chimney breast with its antique-silver-leafed garland is an exact copy of the one in the Salle de Diane at Versailles. While all these outsize elements look perfectly at home in the room, a merely human visitor feels rather like Alice in Wonderland, especially when tucked into one of the roomlike sofas.

This monumental drawing room is saved from pomposity by flashes of wit and informality that counterbalance its magnificence. Most importantly, the walls are covered in a scratch coat, the crushed-stone layer that builders since ancient times have used under the final plaster of a more conventionally finished wall. In keeping with the idea of a civilized ruin, the wall color varies from dark brown to nearly bone. The designer achieved this effect by mixing instant-coffee powder with the plaster, applying it roughly, then turning on the heat full blast so the walls dried unevenly. Near the ceiling, where the air was hottest, the plaster was bleached to palest bone; between the French doors (mostly hidden under a 1963 painting by John Saladino himself) the finish has crackled like a Chinese glaze.

Beyond an arched doorway of wood bleached to match the floors, the normal-height master bedroom doubles as a sitting room and quiet twentieth-century retreat from the transhistorical excitement of the living room. The Fortuny-covered bed is simply made up as a couch; scattered antique Oriental rugs echo the delicate turquoise of its background. John Saladino had intended to paint this room a related pale blue-green but his wife, Virginia, suggested instead the elusive mauve-beige that now seems so inevitable here and in the foyer. Its glossy surface shimmers softly in contrast to the dry roughness of the drawing-room walls. Tall mirrored storage cabinets from John Saladino's furniture collection for Baker Furniture fit neatly here to help organize clutter. This dual-function room adds essential entertaining space to the apartment. It also demands an extremely tidy life-style.

A tranquil and comfortable bath/dressing room finished in water-green marble and sandblasted glass completes this section of the apartment, which, despite its feeling of space and time travel, is not really very large. The Saladinos' son's room and bath open off the far side of the foyer. Teal-green walls and a ceiling paneled in rough-sawn cedar create a cozy country atmosphere. A rare triangular English walnut "pillow-mirror" is a witty addition to a stack of Japanese wood storage chests. A kitchen with cabinets

In dressing room, stained glass windows light the window seat, whose cushions are made up in Lee Jofa fabric.

crafted of the same brushed metal paneling as the front hall includes high-efficiency cooking equipment and a breakfast area walled in enchanting white relief tiles by Martine Vermeulen of Feu-Follet. As one moves through the apartment the contrast and interaction of light and color produce an impression of size far beyond the actual square footage.

Because space is relatively limited, each of the family's objects must have both meaning and beauty. The Italian side of Mr. Saladino shows itself clearly in the living room, which resembles nothing so much as a Roman courtyard, while a Mediterranean warmth is revealed in details like the seventeenth-century marble bust of Cardinal Farnese that reminds its owner of happy student Sundays spent exploring the Palazzo Farnese in Rome. The English side of the family is represented by inherited Hepplewhite chairs, and by a willingness to mix periods and styles as in an English country house. A down-to-earth American sense of humor reminds you that this is a place for fun and relaxation. As the owner himself says, "Some of this is wonderfully fraudulent (like the moving-man's quilt hung as a tapestry), and some is wonderful, but it all works together."

Particular homage is paid to John Saladino's father, a doctor, in the Adam drawing-room carpet with its corner motif of the caduceus, symbol of physicians. This was the first thing bought specifically for the apartment, and the entire color scheme grew out of its muted shades. A very elegant series of visual puns was created by sculptor Mark West, who turned nineteenth-century Pompeian-style bronze tripods into lamps and designed a long shade pull in patinated bronze in ancient Greek style—an object mysterious in function but so beautiful that it hangs on the wall of the foyer. The owner's oldest friend, antiquarian G.R. Durenberger of San Juan Capistrano, contributed the marble hall table supported by one elegantly turned leg that is all that remains of an eighteenth-century stone garden figure.

John Saladino describes this apartment as the culmination of his life and design experience, but he also says, "I like rooms that unfold, like people." It seems safe to guess that, fascinating as it is today, this family home will continue to evolve along with the family whose history and life at this juncture it reflects so beautifully.

Henri Samuel

*H*enri Samuel, whose reputation as one of the major decorators of our era was established virtually from the beginning of his career in Paris in the twenties, comes from a family of visual people who were art dealers, collectors, and bankers. Confident early on that his eye was his gift, Samuel learned the business of interior decoration in the twenties under the legendary Mr. Boudin of Jansen. Starting at the top, he stayed there—though not for long at Jansen—and has worked decade after decade since for a small group of museums and private clients with houses all over Europe as well as for a number of Americans who came across his work in their travels.

Rarely called in to help clients who were starting from scratch, Samuel has usually worked for collectors who have been thinking about architecture and decoration for a long time. So identified is Henri Samuel with the installation of collections and the restoration of historic houses that his reputation as a decorator is rather like that of a poet's poet or an editor's editor. His instincts, preferences, dislikes, and habits speak out to those who are interested in a kind of aesthetic shorthand.

Samuel's unpedantic but correct treatment of important pieces—consummately shown in his Wrightsman and more recently installed Linsky Galleries at the Metropolitan Museum of Art in New York—becomes even more essential when he is doing up houses with collections that could easily look stiff and pompous. One of the ways he saves a house from looking like a museum is to mix furniture and works of art from several periods. His own house in Paris celebrates a rich assortment of eighteenth-, nineteenth-, and twentieth-century furniture and pictures, African and Oriental works of art, grouped by shape, color, and mood and set in a remarkable series of rooms on the ground floor of a late-eighteenth-century *hôtel particulier* in the Faubourg St. Honoré.

One's impression of the place begins on the street. Large wooden doors open from it into a cobbled courtyard. On the other side of the court are a couple of steps, an outer door, and then a pair of gray-white double doors with some ancient fingerprints, a standard indication that something worthwhile lies within. A perfect butler opens the door, and immediately—as though to say that life is as important to the setting as the quality of the furniture and objects—a pair of dachshunds blasts through the entry hall in full voice.

This hall has been made into a green library with Empire furniture, a pair of full-size Empire bookcases, a marble fountain by Carpeaux fitted into a niche as though it were sculpture, a collection of bronzes, contemporary pictures propped up waiting to be hung elsewhere in the house.

Though there is a lot to look at here, the eye moves through and beyond to an enormous drawing room that opens through a series of four double French doors into a big, mostly green, city garden. The big room is hung with material of a color that's a cross between Pompeian red and terra cotta. The walls are covered in a nineteenth-century arrangement of twentieth-century paintings and drawings—a Hartung, a Jawlensky, two canvases by Balthus—and the room is furnished with large clean-lined sofas covered in gray-black velvet. There are also Louis XVI desks and chairs, a bronze table by Diego Giacometti, and other tables and consoles designed for him by contemporary artists such as Guy de Rougemont and César. The length of this room runs parallel to the garden. Across the garden sits a little house of three rooms that make up Henri Samuel's private apartment. His sitting room and bedroom are padded and hung with printed cotton material of his own design and filled with upholstered furniture, Regency and Napoleon III chairs, Directoire tables, nineteenth-century red pottery

Preceding pages:
Green Empire hall-library,
fountain by Carpeaux,
zodiac ceiling painted by
Bores. Left: *A view from*
Henri Samuel's private
apartment across garden
and into drawing room
windows. Above: *One of*
two mahogany bookcases
in the green library. In
foreground, one of a
group of chairs made for
Queen Hortense when
she gave an Aztec ball.

Above: *Henri Samuel's drawing room is renowned for his collection and arrangement of 20th-century art. Le fruit d'or by Balthus hangs over console by César with David Levine drawing, Léger watercolor.* Opposite: *In Samuel's bedroom, walls wear cotton of his design. Chinese paintings on mirror, japanned furniture, Napoleon III chairs.*

made in England, Chinese paintings on mirrored glass, and a set of French 1830 gouaches of Paris, Saint-Cloud, and Versailles. A round three-tiered table displays a collection of ivory, silver, and crystal objects. Large round-topped windows look into the garden and the main house.

The success of this wide-ranging eclecticism results from Samuel's sense of what is suitable for each room. Empire furniture, because it is formal, works well in a room that is both entry hall and library. The dark green that sets it off is a color Empire furniture flourishes against. That it is also a rich dark color in a space receiving little daylight is a result of Samuel's instinct that dark rooms are better off made rich and cozy than painted a white or beige that will look dingy in insufficient sunlight. All of Samuel's modern and contemporary paintings are in the big drawing room

rather than being scattered throughout the house. Chinese paintings that look well with the shiny black of Regency furniture in his bedroom are joined by comfortable tufted Napoleon III chairs. Patterned walls occur only in these small intimate rooms. Samuel's sense of when to use pattern and when not to, when upholstered furniture will add the right note of modernity and comfort in rooms full of fine furniture, why seventeenth-century rather than eighteenth-century furniture looks right in a rustic country castle is a result of years of looking and living. It is his strong sense of what is suitable that prevents him from being swept away by fashion. He is, for instance, no newcomer to the romantic appeal of nineteenth-century interiors, having supervised the restoration of Guy de Rothschild's Château de Ferrières to its original Napoleon III opulence in 1957. He cautions his cli-

ents to buy only the best quality in a century that has been euphorically returned to favor but contains nevertheless the same highs and lows in quality as any other era.

Samuel's own use of nineteenth-century elements is very precise. The early neoclassical part of the nineteenth century he mates with any furniture based on classical antecedents—Louis XIII, Louis XIV, and Louis XVI—in fact with anything but the asymmetrical, unclassical, rococo period of Louis XV or rococo-inspired moments in the Victorian era. English Regency, Napoleon III, and Victorian furniture he uses together because they share a flamboyant mood, are often painted black, and in each case appeared hand-in-glove with revivals of fashionable interest in Oriental things. Though the Empire style is something he has always liked in principle, only some Empire furniture ac-

Above: *Over drawing room's Empire chimney is Balthus's* Strawberries. *To right, a large canvas by Tal Coat. Paintings by Christo and Jawlensky between windows.*
Opposite: *In entrance hall, mobile by Hiquily; Chinese mother-of-pearl pagoda on Directoire table.*

tually finds its way into his life. A few Napoleon III chairs in a bedroom where their eccentricity and comfort is appealing, but not poufs and balloon-backed chairs all over the house. And he resists affecting a high-Victorian clutter just for the sake of living surrounded by a modish accumulation of things.

Henri Samuel's long association with the installation of decorative-arts galleries at the Metropolitan is a tribute to his deep familiarity with period furniture. The wider appreciation of Samuel's treatment of the past is perhaps because of his recognition that "real" period rooms are at best only contemporary fantasies. But that's no disappointment. What's "real" to most people is the mood. And such finely tuned evocations of the past are what have made Henri Samuel's work the cutting edge.

Barbara Schwartz

*I*n 1965, interior designer Barbara Schwartz and her husband, the writer Eugene Schwartz, were "unknown, poor, and fervid," as Mr. Schwartz tells it. "We did not know all that much about art, although we had studied and looked for five years. One day Samuel Kootz was kind enough to guide us around an exhibition of Hans Hofmann. We were immediately attracted to *The Song of the Nightingale*, the biggest, most prominent work in the show, but it was much too expensive for us. The next day I went back—alone, because it was a dangerous mission. I said to Sam, "I'd love to own the painting. Can I give you all the money I have in the world and pay the remainder in monthly payments? If I miss any one of the payments, you can keep the money, take back the painting, and we'll be even.' He looked at me and said, 'You're crazy.' "

The Schwartzes' purchase of the Hofmann is a charming story in retrospect, but to have actually made that precipitous transaction was a hair-raising gamble. Yet plunging into art is not only how they began to collect but how they've continued to amass their collection of modern and contemporary art, a hoard that far exceeds the wall space their New York penthouse generously provides.

The Schwartzes' Hofmann is the Abstract Expressionist cornerstone of their collection. Hofmann's own formal concerns did not prevent him from inspiring others with competing artistic truths, one of which—that

Preceding pages: *Living room's largest canvas is by Jules Olitsky, sculpture in corner by David Smith, painting above sofa by David Salle (with tinkering by Julian Schnabel). Sculpture in foreground, Gary Stephan.* Left: *In another corner, Hans Hoffman's* The Song of the Nightingale, *wall sculpture by Robert Smithson, Robert Graham's* Nude Ascending a Ladder.

the essence of painting is flatness—had a decided influence on the development of Color Field and its distilled practice in certain late works of Morris Louis and his one-time collaborator Kenneth Noland and those of Jules Olitski, all of whom are presented in the Schwartzes' collection.

It is impossible to miss the fine David Smith and Milton Avery prominently displayed in the apartment, but generally speaking, the Schwartzes collected Color Field and Pop in the sixties, figurative painting in the eighties, closely tracking the shifts, dodges, and "right angles the artists make." There is a conspicuous hiatus in the early seventies. Then, they stopped collecting painting because they had overextended themselves. Meanwhile, Mr. Schwartz went to photo galleries with his photographer son, but just to keep him company since the medium left him cold. One day in 1975, however, the vast range of tonality in a George Tice print of a gas station converted him. The next five years were spent buying portraits by Steichen, Strand, Weston, Sander, Walker Evans, and Diane Arbus, photographers remembered for imposing a distinctive style of seeing on the rapt and troubled faces staring back at them.

Meanwhile, in 1978, when a leak in their apartment literally threatened to wash away the stain in the Color Field paintings, the Schwartzes removed them all and, except for a month on view at Knoedler's, the paintings were kept in storage. Depressed by bare walls, the couple commissioned four young painters to decorate four rooms of their apartment, a temporary scheme they liked well enough to let remain for a couple of years.

"Then, in 1980, we discovered the new, rambunctious, outrageous, terrible art—which we immediately loved, and we plunged into paintings again," says Mr. Schwartz. One of the most remarkable works is *Jump.* "It is a two-panel painting that David Salle gave in a trade to Julian Schnabel. When Schnabel got it home he didn't quite like it, so he did a portrait of Salle over the left-hand portion. It became quite notorious. It wasn't for sale the first time I saw it, in Julian's studio—but I seized the opportunity to make my interest known."

Designing an apartment for vast canvases and jutting sculpture presents its own distinct challenge, but Barbara Schwartz has made a specialty of designing environments that, reticent in themselves, throw art into prominence. Against her better business instincts, Barbara Schwartz believes that life in the apartment takes precedence over things she might put there. Her hope is to create environments that allow the inhabitants "to grow and change, and to do so without redecorating."

Clockwise around the entrance are a sculpture by Jonathan Borofsky, a drawing by Robert Longo, and paintings by Kenneth Noland and Milton Avery.

"Easel paintings are easily hung above furniture, but the mural-size paintings of contemporary art take the entire wall, so I move furniture away from the wall and float it in the room," she says. She holds detail low to the ground, so anyone seated can enjoy much decorative finesse, while anyone standing has an unobstructed view of the art on the walls. At that point, "the furniture becomes invisible," she says.

The Schwartzes agree that furniture should be demure and disciplined support for exciting art. "Barbara designs a space that makes the art look good, and I, as the operations manager, supervise the hanging of paintings." Believing stylistic differences do not preclude exhilarating visual connections, the Schwartzes always mix their art.

Where possible, they hang Color Field and neo-Expressionist canvases in one room "to show they're equally valid, equally exploratory, and equally engaging."

About twice a year, the couple reinstalls the entire apartment, removing several paintings and making many major changes. "Oh, yes," Mr. Schwartz says, "last time it took one week and two days to mount it all." The art they remove goes in storage, to friends who'll enjoy it, and sometimes to museums because "when the work is very good, I get to see it all the time." Sometimes, however, pieces go on sale, usually the older art deaccessioned for newer pieces. And the collection keeps changing, while the functional environment in which it sits holds its breath.

In the master bedroom, a lusty Julian Schnabel lords over chevrons by Noland, a monoprint by Adolf Benca, and a box by Lucas Samaras. Armchair from Stendig.

Stephen Sills

I grew up in Durant, Oklahoma, and out there in the country you could create anything you wanted," says designer Stephen Sills. "I could be in a creek bed and fantasize I was on the Nile or walk in the woods and feel like I was in the forest at Versailles." Since those childhood excursions Sills has lived and studied in Paris, spent ten years as a designer in Dallas, and now has a burgeoning business in New York, where he belongs to that group of young designers who experiment with an aesthetic of engaging wit and complex illusion. Fantasy, the sheer romance of the faraway, the magic of antiquity, is only the beginning in Sills's work. Beyond the stark mural façade of his two-story Dallas town house—he spent two years gutting and rebuilding this "laboratory" for his visual inventions—the rich furnishings and coolly classical proportions inspire the mood of an eighteenth-century Italian villa. Yet the historicism is at times authentic, at times teasingly fraudulent; illusion and reality cross tracks so often that the eye soon learns to assume nothing and imagine anything.

The acknowledged leitmotiv for this ambitious design foray is the stunningly eccentric wall treatment in the living room. Here Sills draped plaster-dipped muslin, which after hundreds of painstaking coats of wet plas-

Preceding pages: *Living room as grotto. Plaster-coated draped muslin provides a faux-stone backdrop for Roman antiquities, Louis XVI table, gilt chairs from Chatsworth in Old World Weavers satin, and a Viennese Deco lamp on a silver Mughal side table. Polka dots and Clarence House stripes add a contemporary insouciance.* Left: *Swedish neoclassical chairs were upholstered in leather painted to resemble stone. Columns found in a Paris flea market.*

ter has assumed the texture and apparent substance of cut stone. It's a brilliantly contemporary faux conceit, but in its evocation of fossilized antiquity—one thinks of drapery for an enormous classical Greek sculpture—it is also a subtle reference to the archaeological craze that so influenced eighteenth-century styles. This faux tour de force sets up a fine collection of bona fide Roman antiquities, the statuary fragments, freestanding fluted columns, and statuettes of swirling draped goddesses that any thoroughly modern eighteenth-century collector would have coveted. To these Sills has added such period antiques as an elegantly spare Louis XVI mahogany table and a set of François Hervé gilt chairs from Chatsworth, upholstered in cobalt-blue satin. Still more historical scope, and ambiguity, is provided by such late-modern flourishes as a large blue glass cube—made by Sills from the windows of an old Dallas candy store—that resembles a piece by Donald Judd, or the gray, fixtureless, wall-to-ceiling living room double doors that hang with the ponderous yet carefully balanced simplicity of a Richard Serra sculpture.

An ardent devotee of neoclassicism, Sills has arranged his interior with appropriate restraint—he likes clarity, not clutter—but a streak of baroque exuberance emerges in his eye-challenging use of materials. The ceiling of his living room is covered with Japanese silver tea paper

*Entry hall combines
unglazed Islamic tiles,
18th-century Irish mirror
and bracket, Chinese
porcelain, Egyptian
alabaster, and French
Deco furnishings,
including Jean Michel
Frank parchment cabinet.*

that strongly suggests sheet metal, and the living room floor is paved in marble cut and laid like brick. Sills has been fascinated with trompe-l'oeil painting ever since childhood, so not surprisingly he has become a virtuoso of faux. His special effects range from outrageous to flawlessly counterfeit. The tortoiseshell baseboard in his bedroom is a good example of the former; his stairs—the risers are faux marbre and the steps the real thing—defy the eye to make a distinction.

Sills's trompe-l'oeil technique is so deft that he can even pounce with confidence on the accidents of the creative process. The bookcases and closets he built in his upstairs library were originally intended to imitate bleached terra cotta, but as Sills painted away he realized he was getting something that looked like leather. The finished effect not only complements the leather-uphol-stered neoclassical chairs but adds a lived-in warmth and a sense of old-world richness. And in Sills's domain even deception may be wrapped in deception. The entry hall appears to be painted to resemble massive limestone blocks. Closer inspection reveals that the stone is indeed faux, but so is the trompe-l'oeil painting; the surface is actually unretouched wallpaper cut into squares and pasted over a "mortar" of plain brown wallpaper.

Not content to stop at two-dimensional trickery, Sills also enjoys spatial legerdemain. He has extended his "draped" living room wall into the garden by several feet, and the outside portion is visible through floor-to-ceiling glass doors. The eye initially perceives the section of wall outside as a reflection in mirrored glass, information that is subsequently, with cubist logic, denied by the view of the garden through the bogus "mirror." Even more confounding is the startling artifice Sills set up in the library. Behind the half-wall overlooking the entry hall Sills has hung a large mirror in a massive French Art Deco frame finished in tarnished gold Korean lacquer. Set atop the half-wall are two nineteenth-century architectural models representing sections of Roman buildings. When seated in the library one immediately sees their reflection, backed by the antique architecture of the library, in the smoky, slightly distorting glass, and from there it is a short step into a vista that might have been seen through a window in eighteenth-century Rome. Now completely enthralled with this culminating vision, the intellect finally concedes what the eye has been telling it all along, that from the streets of twentieth-century Dallas to those of eighteenth-century Rome is only as far as Stephen Sills, designer, connoisseur, and conjurer, wants it to be.

Faux stones in entry are actually cut wallpaper over another paper ground. Sills opened up the staircase wall, which originally went straight up to ceiling, and added marble floors.

Left: *In the library,
leather-look cornices
support specially cast
stone finials. Reflection
of architectural models in
the Korean lacquer Deco
mirror suggests a window
into time.* Above: *Sills
built the alcove for a
guest bed covered with
rare English paisley and
flanked by Italian
neoclassical chairs.*

John Stefanidis

Chelsea is a fashionable and romantic London district on the north side of the Thames whose houses bear more than the usual number of blue-enameled historic markers stating that this or that luminary once lived there. The list of former Chelsea residents includes monarchs, a saint, and many artists: Richard III lived here as a Duke in 1483. Thomas More settled in Chelsea in 1520 and played host to Erasmus and Holbein here. Henry VIII built a Chelsea manor house where Elizabeth I probably lived between her mother's and her father's deaths. Writers Thomas Carlyle, George Eliot, George Meredith, and Oscar Wilde had houses in the district, as did painters Turner, Sargent, and Whistler.

Whistler inhabited part of the only seventeenth-century great house that still stands in Chelsea, although the building was subdivided in the eighteenth century and now consists of three town houses. It is in Whistler's old Cheyne Walk quarters on the riverfront that the London-based international interior designer John Stefanidis lives.

Stefanidis is not immune to the historical glamour of his 1674 house. "The building stands on the site of Sir Thomas More's farm," he says, "and I look out my

Above: *In the sitting
room, a 20th-century
bronze vase and Japanese
candlesticks stand on an
18th-century Venetian
chest.* Opposite: *Besides
the formal dining room,
there is this less formal
dining setting in the
drawing room's
sunny bay.*

window at the same view Whistler so often sketched and painted." But it was his designer's eye that convinced Stefanidis to move here, where the rooms are large and tall and beautifully detailed and daylight streams through from morning till night. "The sparkling river light was irresistible," he recalls, adding, "Light is the first thing I perceive when I visit a new place."

John Stefanidis is known for his gentle way with rooms and houses and, indeed, with clients. He doesn't have a personal stamp that he feels he must set upon his every work. If a decorating connoisseur were able to spot a Stefanidis room in a flash, this discreet designer would feel he had done something wrong.

The spirit of the place is what concerns him most, for that determines his design, in the country or in town. At his weekend house, which Stefanidis built out of tumble-down cowsheds, floors are brick, rough trusses are exposed. "No parquet floors or gessoed ceilings there," he explains. "That's for another kind of country house." When furnishing a London mews flat, Stefanidis is always properly modest and cozy. In his own Chelsea house, built for a lord, he moved nobly through the noble spaces, placing excellent antiques, works of art, rugs and chandeliers, but without a shadow of pretentiousness.

Sense of place is one Stefanidis strength. He is also appreciated for his subtle sense of color, playing variations on soft neutral shades so skillfully that no feeling of monotony results. Another strong point is his way with scale, which he may bring up or down, the latter best seen in his own dining room, where guests in a twenty-foot-tall space sit convivially under ceilings lowered by a double frieze of pictures and a chandelier. Comfort is a constant Stefanidis preoccupation in rooms of any size or degree of formality: he designs almost all the upholstered furniture that appears in his rooms and plans it dimensionally and materially for the greatest ease.

How does it all add up on Cheyne Walk? The comment of a young visitor so pleased her host that he was willing to share it: "Whenever I come here, I feel I am in the right place." He hopes all his guests feel this way.

A Regency chaise longue
stands at the foot of a
Regency fourposter bed
hung in Stefanidis fabric.
The large oil painting of
Medici lap dogs is by
Jacopo da Empoli.
Cabinet of spaced dowels
with glass top is by
Stefanidis. Venetian mask
in foreground hangs on a
cheval-glass column.

Grateful acknowledgment is made to the following photographers and writers for permission to reprint photographs and articles previously published in *House & Garden* Magazine.

Photographers

Ernst Beadle, 226–231

Adam Bartos, 70–77

Langdon Clay, 24–31

Edgar de Evia, Front Jacket, 32–37, 196–203

Carla di Bendetti, 134–143, Back Jacket

Jacques Dirand, 12–23, 220–225

Feliciano, 5, 52–59, 104–111

Oberto Gili, 60–69, 78–83, 94–103, 112–121, 176–185, 186–195, 232–237, 248–255, 280–287

Mick Hales, 162–167

Mary Harty and Peter de Rosa, 46–51

François Halard, 2, 84–93, 256–265, 288–295

Timothy Hursley, 152–159

Grant Mudford, 144–151, 296

Mary E. Nichols, 274–279

Karen Radkai, 38–45, 122–133, 168–175, 204–213, 266–273

William P. Steele, 214–219

Writers

Steven M. L. Aronson, 94–103, 176–185

Rosamond Bernier, 38–45, 186–195

Mary Cantwell, 214–219

Michael Ennis, 280–287

Martin Filler, 144–151

Jean Garvin, 70–77

Lisa Germany, 104–111

Alice Gordon, 112–121, 204–213

Elaine Greene, 24–31, 46–51, 162–167, 168–175, 220–225, 232–237, 288–295

Fayal Greene, 256–265

Lois Wagner Greene, 152–159

Christopher Hemphill, 122–133, 226–231

Jesse Kornbluth, 78–83

Alan Pryce-Jones, 248–255

John Richardson, 12–23, 60–69, 84–93

Nancy Richardson, 266–273

Paul Schmidt, 196–203

Nina A. Straight, 52–59

Isa Vercelloni, 134–143

Marjorie Welish, 274–279

Gabrielle Winkel, 32–37

Opposite: *Bar in front of window in Harry Hunt's apartment in San Francisco, decorated by Andrée Putman.*

Index

The text of this book
was set in Simoncini Garamond by the Composition Department
of Condé Nast Publications, Inc.
The four-color separations were done by The Color Company.
The book was printed and bound
by W. A. Krueger, Company.
Text paper is 80-pound Patina Matte.